HINDUISM

IS VOLUME

144

OF THE

Twentieth Century Encyclopedia of Catholicism

UNDER SECTION

XIV

NON-CHRISTIAN BELIEFS

IT IS ALSO THE

24TH

VOLUME IN ORDER OF PUBLICATION

THE TWENTIETH CENTURY ENCYCLOPEDIA OF CATHOLICISM

Edited by HENRI DANIEL-ROPS of the Académie Française

HINDUISM

By *SOLANGE LEMAÎTRE*

Translated from the French by *JOHN-FRANCIS BROWN*

HAWTHORN BOOKS · PUBLISHERS · *New York*

 This book was manufactured in the United States of America and published simultaneously in Canada by McClelland & Stewart, Ltd., 25 Hollinger Road, Toronto 16. It was originally published in France under the title, *Hindouisme ou Sanâtana Dharma.* © Librairie Arthème Fayard, 1957. The Library of Congress has catalogued The Twentieth Century Encyclopedia of Catholicism under card number 58-14327. Library of Congress Catalogue Card No. for this volume: 59-12165. The Catholic University of America Library has catalogued this volume based on the Lynn-Peterson Alternative Classification for Catholic Books: BQT 184. J43v. 144/BL 1201.

First Edition, August, 1959

NIHIL OBSTAT

Hubertus Richards, S.T.L., L.S.S.

Censor Deputatus

IMPRIMATUR

E. Morrogh Bernard

Vicarius Generalis

Westmonasterii, die XVII APRILIS MCMLIX

CONTENTS

INTRODUCTION

Before sketching a brief outline of the Hindu religion in space too short for so vast a subject, I should like first to thank those Indian and French friends whose works have been of assistance to me in preparing this book. I should also like to justify the title of this work.

There is no single religion in India but rather a combination of related religions, representing different facets of the Vedic "tradition", which is the initial source of the sects that, without being mutually incompatible, have developed on Indian soil.

To give clarity to my account, I have chosen not to make an historical division of the subject, but to treat it as a whole derived from the Vedic revelation. In dealing with its origins, I shall call it the Vedic religion and thereafter the Sanātana Dharma, which is in fact the name for the religious tradition and the only name current in India for the religions that belong to this tradition and are described here. But since the term "Hinduism" is generally used by European Indologists, I have kept it to denote the subject of this book.

The civilization of India, at root purely religious, is only now becoming known in Europe; and as the mystery surrounding it is unveiled it emerges as one of the highest achievements in the history of mankind. By the very breadth of the outlook it affords on to the destiny of man the Vedic religion offers in abundance the spiritual experience that has inspired the Indian people since the dawn of their history. "The vocation of India is to proclaim to the world the efficacy of religious experience."

Little is known of the beginnings of Indian civilization which stretch into prehistoric obscurity. European scholars have suggested many dates but, in the present state of knowledge, they have been unable to agree on an exact dating for the first stages of this civilization. Seen by its initiates as the result of a divine revelation, occurring considerably before the historic period, the Vedic religion, as found in the hymns of the Vedas, overshadows the life of India in its entirety from the very beginnings down to the present day. This is due to the permanence of its basic religious and philosophical tradition, despite the evolutions its forms have undergone and whatever its name as it passed through history in the sects that it engendered.

And once it has been revealed, the truth received by the ṛṣis cannot change. For this truth is holy knowledge ("Veda" being "knowledge" *par excellence*), written deep into the Vedas, the sacred books of the Vedic religion.

The contents of the Vedic texts were aurally received (*śruti* means "hearing"), emanating from Brahman, "breathed out by Brahman in the form of words". The ṛṣis, inspired sages, who received these words by a direct hearing, were seers, endowed with a supreme intuition as "see-ers" of an eternal truth.

Vedic revelation proclaims a unity. When once this concept was metaphysically established, the idea of the One—of necessity always identical with itself—as the fount of all plurality came to serve as the definitive basis of all Indian religion, as well as of the unity of Hinduism, a purely traditional fact, needing no other confirmation than that of its own doctrine.

The Vedic ideal was to be the pure spring from which all India drew to water a civilization that was to grow and change as different ages and different regions demanded.

For India is a veritable continent, almost as large as Europe in its extent and in the numerical importance of its population. It holds so great a number of races, languages and religions that quite deep divergences and oppositions of all sorts could not fail to appear in an evolution spread over thousands of years. But the idea of the Absolute was then and still is the fundamental attitude of Indian philosophy, despite the innumerable forms of religion that coexist within the Sanātana Dharma or Hinduism; with the result that it faces the passage of human events with a serene imperturbability. Hence it is understandable that neither history nor chronology held much importance for the Hindu mind.

S. L.

CHAPTER I

THE VEDAS

The Vedic religion constitutes our starting-point as the most ancient form of Indian religious tradition—the Sanātana Dharma or, as most European Indologists would call it, Hinduism.

In those almost legendary prehistoric times, human thought functioned in ways far removed from ours. It preferred to express itself in images, in symbols that are hard enough to translate and even harder to interpret. An exact idea of what this religion meant to its adherents is now difficult to obtain. It is even to be wondered whether the teachings of the Veda were deliberately obscured against the understanding of the layman so as to hide from him their inner meaning. Indeed, was not one of the essential points of Vedic instruction precisely this sacred and secret nature of knowledge—the knowledge of the self and the true mystery of the gods? This knowledge could be dangerous to minds unprepared to receive it by bringing in its train a misinterpretation or a misuse of it.

No doubt there was an external cult intended for the public as well as an internal discipline reserved to the initiate. Thus we have hymns from the Vedas that have an immediate and concrete application to the demands of ritual, while at the same time containing a secret meaning within their hieratic formulas. Only "those whose soul is pure and mind prepared are able to 'hear' the secret of the words pronounced in the 'right manner' ".

Śrī Aurobindo has written that the figure of speech "śleṣa", a rhetorical device based on ambiguity of verbal meaning, is traditional in Sanskrit Vedic literature and that the esoteric Vedic teaching holds key-words—important words of double, or even multiple, meaning. For the ṛṣi "speech", or the Word, is a living thing, a power of creation. "It is not yet the conventional symbol of an idea, but the shaper, the generator of the idea." The sound of a word, moreover, had a value whose extent is hard to assess.

In considering the Vedas, it must be remembered that one is in the presence of a world of mysteries which for the most part are barely approachable, profound mysteries with a symbolism obscure to the majority of those that read them without training.

On the one hand, European Indologists, by their great works of erudition, have shed the light of their scholarship on controversial problems, while on the other, certain Hindu scholars like Śrī Aurobindo have devoted themselves to the quest of the "secret" of the Veda by recourse to a specifically Indian intuition.

There is more than a purely literal meaning to be found in the Vedas. This can be felt behind the poetic imagery of many hymns about the Creation and the Divine, in which certain lines sparkle like specks of gold in the opacity of their vein. These specks of gold herald the mine, with its uncovered treasures and those, still to be found which, though buried, will gradually come to the light of day. The Vedic hymns invite a deeper investigation before they can yield the whole of their true meaning.

According to Śrī Aurobindo[1]:

> The central conception of the Veda is the conquest of the Truth out of the darkness of Ignorance and by the conquest of the Truth the conquest also of Immortality. For the Vedic *Ṛtam* is a spiritual as well as a psychological conception. It is the true being, the true consciousness, the true delight of existence beyond this earth of body, this mid-region of vital force, this ordinary sky or heaven of mind. We have to cross beyond all these planes in order to arrive at the higher plane of that superconscient Truth which is the own home of the gods and the foundation of Immortality. This is the world of Swar, to which the Aṅgirasas have found the path for their prosperity.

[1] Śrī Aurobindo, *On the Veda*, p. 277 ff.

The Aṅgirasas are at once the divine seers who assist in the cosmic and human workings of the gods and their earthly representatives, the ancient fathers who first found the wisdom of which the Vedic hymns are a chant and memory and renewal in experience. [. . .]

Usha is the divine Dawn, for the Sun that arises by her coming is the Sun of the superconscient Truth. . . . Usha herself is the Truth, *sūnṛtā*, and the mother of Truths. These truths of the divine Dawn are called her cows, her shining herds; while the forces of the Truth that accompany them and occupy the Life are called her horses. Around this symbol of the cows and horses much of the Vedic symbolism turns; for these are the chief elements of the riches sought by man from the gods. The cows of the Dawn have been stolen and concealed by the demons, the lords of darkness in their nether cave of the secret subconscient. They are the illuminations of knowledge, the thoughts of the Truth, *gāvo matayaḥ*, which have to be delivered out of their imprisonment. Their release is the upsurging of the powers of the divine Dawn.

This is Śrī Aurobindo's conclusion on the Rigveda:

From the historical point of view the Rig-veda may be regarded as a record of a great advance made by humanity by special means at a certain period of its collective progress. In its esoteric, as well as its exoteric significance, it is the Book of Works, of the inner and the outer sacrifice; it is the spirit's hymn of battle and victory as it discovers and climbs to planes of thought and experience inaccessible to the natural or animal man, man's praise of the divine Light, Power and Grace at work in the mortal.

[The present version of the Veda] is perhaps only the last testament of the Ages of Intuition, the luminous Dawns of the Forefathers, to their descendants, to a human race already turning in spirit towards the lower levels and the more easy and secure gains —secure perhaps only in appearance—of the physical life and of the intellect and the logical reason.

But these are only speculations and inferences. Certain it is that the old tradition of a progressive obscuration and loss of the Veda as the law of the human cycle has been fully justified by the event. The obscuration had already proceeded far before the opening of the next great age of Indian spirituality, the Vedantic, which struggled to preserve or recover what it yet could of the ancient knowledge.[2]

[2] Śrī Aurobindo, *ibid.*, p. 12 ff.

CHAPTER II

THE TEXTS

The texts of the Vedas vary in date and inspiration and constitute the only evidence available to us in translation bearing on the Vedic religion. They make up a vast body of material and together provide the most ancient monument of Indian religious and cosmogonical ideas.

This literature, written in an archaic dialect of Sanskrit, is exceptional in that its origins and preservation have been purely oral. Its transmission has continued without interruption from generation to generation—"from mouth to ear"—in the strictest possible way and even today is accomplished in this fashion, despite the existence of written versions.

According to Renou, "the most ancient manuscripts have no more value than the testimony of men, who until recently carried in their memories repertoires of varying length from the Veda.

"From the moment it was fixed, the text was preserved with a quite amazing fidelity. By reciting the Pada text and other more complicated versions that came to be added later, by means of the minute phonetic descriptions of which an example is preserved in the Ṛkprātiśākhya, the Rigveda has survived in the very form in which the diasceuasts had cast it, without any alteration or variant" (*L'Inde classique*, p. 276).

The most ancient Vedic texts are made up of four collections or saṁhitās and it is they that are known as the Vedas. These four Vedas contain the Śruti or revelation "received" by the ṛṣis. The term "Vedic" is also applied more broadly to bodies of literature based on one or other of these saṁhitās.

The Śruti contains four separate Vedas: the Rigveda, the

Sāmaveda, the Yajurveda (of which there are two recensions called the "Black" and the "White") and the Atharvaveda. Also held to be part of the Śruti are the Brāhmaṇas, prose treatises that interpret Brahman, paying special attention to rites and sacrifices. Each Veda has several of these Brāhmaṇas, with the exception of the Atharvaveda. Secondly after the Brāhmaṇas, we have the Āraṇyakas or "forest-teachings", and thirdly the Upaniṣads, which are esoteric philosophical treatises held to be part of Śruti.

Under the title of Smṛti are gathered other Vedic documents which constitute the "tradition by memory". These are:

1. The Sūtras or collections of aphorisms bearing on ceremonial or domestic ritual.

2. The Dharmaśāstra, manuals of canon, civil and criminal law compiled by inspired law-givers.

3. The Itihāsas or great epic poems devoted to the lives of certain heroes. The Bhagavadgītā, which is part of one of these great poems, is held, as an exception, to be Śruti.

4. The Purāṇas or "ancient traditional histories", an assemblage of all the legends that have accumulated about certain deities. Sometimes the Purāṇas are grouped with a class of similar works that are called Tantras—"Books". These belong to the form of Hinduism known as "Tantrism".

Although they are not strictly part of Smṛti, certain devotional works or mystic poems and even some commentaries on the sacred texts are assembled under this title.

THE RIGVEDA

The Rigveda, or "verse-Veda", the oldest document in all Indian literature, contains about a thousand hymns divided into ten "circles" or maṇḍalas. These hymns are prayers or works of praise addressed to the gods, in particular to Indra, Agni and later to Prajāpati.

It is a much-wrought, literary work, abounding in techniques of allusion. But the chief importance of these texts that deal with the ritual forms of the cult is that they embody the first speculations of the philosophy that was to have such a considerable metaphysical development in India.

For Śrī Aurobindo, the Rigveda is a whole in all its parts. "Whichever of its ten maṇḍalas we choose, we find in it the same ideas, the same substance, the same images and the same mannerisms of speech. The ṛṣis are the seers of a single Truth and in order to express it they use a common language" (*ibid.*).

The Vedic hymns, these works of praise addressed to the gods, are miraculous in the magic power of their sonority. They were recited in accordance with inflexible laws by officiants at the solemn sacrifice, either as sung invocations or as murmured prayers, so that those who had ordered these solemn ceremonies of the cult might, by the efficacy of the mantras, attain communion with the "essence of things".

It is in the tenth and last maṇḍala of the Rigveda that are to be found not only the great Creation Hymn with its grandiose lyricism, but also the hymn of the sacrifice of Puruṣa. This conception of the sacrifice, corner-stone of the Hindu religion, established a parallelism between human sacrifice and its divine prototype and links it by analogy to the natural sacrifices of the sky and the elements in the atmosphere.

Certain hymns are devoted to the sacraments of marriage, of which the divine exemplar is that of the sun and moon. Others are concerned with funerals and their accompanying rites and others again belong to the cults of soma and the sacrificial fire. Here are three hymns from the Rigveda.

Funeral hymn

[Invocation to Death, who has taken his victim, to leave the living in peace:]

1. Keep to yonder path that is thine, O Death, and is not the path of the gods. I say to thee who hast eyes and dost hear: harm not our children or our men.

[The living are invited to purify themselves and to cast off their sorrow:]

2. When ye return, effacing the footsteps of Death, continuing further your lives, rich in progeny and possessions, become ye then pure and holy, O worshippers.

3. The living here are divided from the dead. Our plea to the gods has now borne fruit; here have we come for dancing and mirth, continuing further our lives.

[Farewell is said to the dead and the Earth is invoked:]

10. Go unto the Earth, thy mother, this generous Earth of wide expanse, this maiden soft as wool to them that give her a rich reward. May she preserve you in the midst of extinction.

11. O Earth, be thou as a vault above him, do not crush him, be of easy access and offer him a safe retreat. As a mother her son, cover him, O Earth, with the hem of thy garment.

12. When she hath made herself as a vault, may the Earth remain thus, upheld by a thousand pillars. May that dwelling flow with butter for him and serve him ever as a place of refuge.

13. Above thee I make firm the soil, levelling the clod. Let me not be bruised; may the Fathers sustain this pillar and Yama here construct thy dwelling.

[The dead man speaks:]

14. At nightfall they have laid me down like a feather in the arrow. I have drawn in my voice which was falling, as if it were a horse with the reins.

(Rigveda X. 18.)

A cosmogonic hymn

1. There was neither being nor non-being at that time. There was neither space nor the firmament beyond. What was contained therein? What was it? Under whose protection? Where was the deep water, the fathomless water?

2. There was neither death nor non-death at that time, for no sign divided night from day. The One breathed without breath, of its own motion; beyond it nothing else was.

3. In the beginning the shadows covered the shadows, and this all was but indistinguishable water. Enclosed within the void, that which was coming into being, the One, arose then by the power of heat.

4. First desire evolved, the first seed of thought. Wise men, seeking with wisdom in their souls, found in non-being the link of being.

5. Their cord was stretched across; what was above, what was below? There were impregnators, there were powers; there was energy below, there was impulse above.

6. Who truly knows, who could here declare whence was born, whence comes this creation? The gods came after this act of creation; who knows then whence it has arisen?

7. This creation, whence it has arisen, whether it has been made or whether it has not been made—he who watches over it from the summit of heaven knows this certainly, or else he does not know.

(Rigveda X. 129.)

HYMNS AND PRAYERS OF THE VEDA

The primordial god, creator of the world

1. In the beginning the golden embryo grew. Once born it became the sole lord of creation. He sustained this heaven and earth. Who is this god, that we might serve him with our oblation?

2. He who gives life and strength, whose commands all, even the gods, obey; he of whom death and non-death are but the shadow. Who is this god that we might serve him with our oblation?

3. He who by his power has become the sole king of animate things, of all which breathes and sleeps; he who rules the two-footed and four-footed things. Who is this god, that we might serve him with our oblation?

4. He by whose power exist these snowy mountains, the ocean with its Rasā, so they say, and the poles of heaven which are his arms. Who is this god, that we might serve him with our oblation?

5. He who made firm stout heaven and earth, who fixed the sun and the vault of the sky, who measures out space in the atmosphere. Who is this god, that we might serve him with our oblation?

6. Him to whom look for aid the two armies bound to the earth and trembling in their minds; he upon whom the rising sun sheds light. Who is this god, that we might serve him with our oblation?

7. When the great waters came, bearing the universe as an embryo, engendering Agni, then evolved the One, the life-breath of the gods. Who is this god, that we might serve him with our oblation?

8. He who by his power encompassed the waters with his glance, the waters bearing energy and engendering the sacrifice; he who

amongst the gods was the sole god. Who is this god, that we might serve him with our oblation?

9. May the author of the earth not harm us, he who engendered heaven and whose laws are true; he who created the great and sparkling waters. Who is this god, that we might serve him with our oblation?

10. O Prajāpati, it is thou and none other that dost encompass all these created beings. May that which we desire in our offering to thee fall to our lot. May we become lords of wealth.

(Rigveda X. 121.)

The Yajurveda or "Veda of the sacrificial formulas"

The saṁhitās of the Yajurveda are five in number and are divided as follows. The White Yajurveda contains only one saṁhitā, that of the sacrificial and sacred formulas, i.e. of mantras, while the Black Yajurveda contains the other four saṁhitās and adds various exegeses in prose to the original body of liturgical formulas. It is equal in length to about two thirds of the Rigveda. The Yajurveda is a collection of invocations addressed not only to the gods, but also to the cultic objects that acquire from these invocations a sacred character.

The yajus describe summarily that which can be attained by it (the cultic object), urge it to action or impel some other object to come into a connection with it (Oldenberg). They are also prayers in that they express the result that the rite will produce. "The waters have joined with the waters and the plants with the sap. Ye wealthy ones, join with them that are in motion, let the soft come unto the soft." "Thou art the thousand-pointed right arm of Indra with a thousand brightnesses." "By the impulse of his strength, by raising me hath he raised me, verily Indra hath made mine enemies humble by laying them low." "O that I might see the sun, that lighteth unto all men." "Thou art the preservation of Viṣṇu, the shield of the sacrificer: be thou a guard for me." (Renou, *L'Inde classique*, p. 281.)

In certain yajus are found magical elements and others resemble litanies. But on the whole the order of the mantras agrees with that of the ceremony. Here is an extract from the

White Yajurveda in the Maitrāyaṇī saṁhitā, so called from its recension by the Maitrāyaṇīya school, entitled *To Rudra:*

1. Honour to thy wrath, O Rudra, and honour to thine arrow. Honour to thy bow and honour to thy two arms.

2. Friendly are thy forms that look not to terrify or do evil. With thy most beneficent form regard us kindly, O thou that hauntest the mountains.

3. Make friendly the arrow that thou bearest in thy hand, ready to shoot, O lord of the mountain. Harm thou no man nor anything living.

4. We greet thee, lord of the mountain, with friendly speech. Let now all the people be well-disposed to us at the gathering.

5. The advocate has spoken for us, the first healer of the gods. Crushing all serpents, hurl down all witches and frighten them away.

6. He that is dark, ruddy and brown and most auspicious and those Rudras that dwell round about in these regions by the thousands—we conciliate the anger of them all.

7. He that has a blue neck and is red approaches us unawares—the herdsmen have seen him and the girls carrying water; all creatures have seen him—and now that he is seen, let him have mercy on us.

8. Honour to him, with his blue hair and a thousand eyes, for he is generous. Likewise have I paid honour to his warriors.

(MS. II. 9. ii.)

The hymn to Thought is from the Vājasaneyisaṁhitā of the Yajurveda:

1. The divinity that rises far when man is awake and falls back into him when he is asleep, the far-travelling light of lights is Thought. May it be friendly to me in what it devises.

2. That thought with which the wise skilfully perform their tasks in the sacrifice and in the rites—an unheard of wonder within all creatures—is Thought. May it be friendly to me in what it devises.

3. That which is knowledge, consciousness and will, an immortal light within living creatures, without which no action can be performed: such is Thought. May it be friendly to me in what it devises.

4. That which immortally encompasses all that was, is and shall be, by which the sacrifice is performed with the seven officiants is Thought. May it be friendly to me in what it devises.

5. In it are the verses, melodies and formulas like spokes in a car's nave; in it all the thinking of creatures is woven. Such is Thought. May it be friendly to me in what it devises.

6. Driving men as one drives swift steeds with the reins like a skilful charioteer; dwelling in the heart, yet moving and most rapid, such is Thought. May it be friendly to me in what it devises.

(VS. XXXIV. 1–6.)

The Sāmaveda

The Sāmaveda or "Veda of melodies" owes the most part of its verses to the Rigveda, but these verses are accompanied by a musical notation for the performance of the sacred chant and this is its most interesting feature. It contains four gaṇas or groups of chants. Certain isolated tunes or sāmans are sung prayers. A large number of these derive from popular songs.

The Atharvaveda

The Atharvaveda, which also has its resemblances with the Rigveda, is made up of a collection of hymns and spells in twenty books or kāṇḍas (731 sections and nearly 6,000 verses). It is held to be somewhat inferior to the other Vedas, although some prayers have a solemn and poetic ring which is not without grandeur. The hymn to the Earth has real majesty. Its antiquity makes it of special interest to the ethnologist.

A large number of hymns are divided between magic and philosophy, under the guise of incantations. In these hymns can be found the beginnings of Indian medicine with therapeutic formulas serving definite purposes such as the removal of illness, of diabolical possession and the like as well as magical prayers.

Hymn or prayer against fever (*takman*)

1. May Agni drive the takman away from here, may Soma, the press-stone, and Varuṇa, of tried skill; may the altar, the straw (upon the altar), and the brightly-flaming fagots (drive him away)! Away to naught shall go the hateful powers.

2. Thou that makest all men sallow, inflaming them like a searing fire, even now, O takman, thou shalt become void of strength: do thou now go away down, aye, into the depths.

3. The takman that is spotted, covered with spots, like reddish sediment, him thou, (O plant) of unremitting potency, drive away down below.

4. Having made obeisance to the takman, I cast him down below. . . .

12. O takman, along with thy brother balāsa, along with thy sister cough, along with thy cousin pāman, go to yonder foreign folk.

13. Destroy the takman that returns on (each) third day, the one that intermits (each) third day, the one that continues without intermission, and the autumnal one; destroy the cold takman, the hot, him that comes in summer, and him that arrives in the rainy season.
(AV. V. 22.)

Hymn to goddess Earth

1. Truth, greatness, universal order (ṛta), strength, consecration, creative fervour (tapas), spiritual exaltation (brahma), the sacrifice, support the earth. May this earth, the mistress of that which was and shall be, prepare for us a broad domain.

2. The earth that has heights, and slopes, and great plains, that supports the plants of manifold virtue, free from the pressure that comes from the midst of men, she shall spread out for us, and fit herself for us.

3. The earth upon which the sea, and the rivers and the waters, upon which food and the tribes of men have arisen, upon which this breathing, moving life exists, shall afford us precedence in drinking.

4. The earth whose are the four regions of space, upon which food and the tribes of men have arisen, which supports the manifold breathing, moving things, shall afford us cattle and other possessions also.

6. The earth that supports all, furnishes wealth, the foundation, the golden-breasted resting-place of all living creatures, she that supports Agni Vaiśvānara (the fire), and mates with Indra, the bull, shall furnish us with property.

8. The earth which formerly was water upon the ocean (of space), which the wise (seers) found out by their skilful devices; whose heart is in the highest heaven, immortal, surrounded by truth, shall bestow upon us brilliancy and strength, (and place us) in supreme sovereignty.

15. The mortals born of thee live on thee, thou supportest both

bipeds and quadrupeds. Thine, O earth, are these five races of men, the mortals, upon whom the rising sun sheds undying light with his rays.

19. Agni (fire) is in the earth, in the plants, the waters hold Agni, Agni is in the stones; Agni is within men, Agnis (fires) are within cattle, within horses.

29. To the pure earth I speak, to the ground, the soil that has grown through the brahma (spiritual exaltation). Upon thee, that holdest nourishment, prosperity, food, and ghee, we would settle down, O earth.

47. Thy many paths upon which people go, thy tracks for chariots and wagons to advance, upon which both good and evil men proceed, this road, free from enemies, and free from thieves, may we gain: with what is auspicious (on thee) be gracious to us.

60. She whom Viśvakarman (the creator of all) did search out by means of oblations, when she had entered the surging (flood of the) atmosphere, she, the vessel destined to nourish, deposited in a secret place, became visible (to the gods) and the (heavenly) mothers.

(AV. XII. 1.)

Beginning of a hymn to Varuṇa

1. The great guardian among these (gods) sees as if from anear. He that thinketh he is moving stealthily—all this the gods know.

2. If a man stands, walks, or sneaks about, if he goes slinking away, if he goes into his hiding-place; if two persons sit together and scheme, king Varuṇa is there as a third, and knows it.

3. Both this earth here belongs to king Varuṇa, and also yonder broad sky whose boundaries are far away. Moreover these two oceans are the loins of Varuṇa; yea, he is hidden in this small (drop of) water.

4. He that should flee beyond the heaven far away would not be free from king Varuṇa. His spies come hither (to the earth) from heaven, with a thousand eyes do they watch over the earth.

5. King Varuṇa sees through all that is between heaven and earth, and all that is beyond. He has counted the winkings of men's eyes. As a (winning) gamester puts down his dice, thus does he establish these (laws).

(AV. IV. 16. i–v.)[1]

[1] Trans. M. Bloomfield, *Hymns of the Atharva-Veda* (Sacred Books of the East, XLII), published by the Clarendon Press, Oxford.

CHAPTER III

THE BRĀHMAṆAS

The Brāhmaṇas are prose commentaries devoted to theological interpretations of Brahman by means of symbols and concerned with sacred lore through its explanation of rites and formulas. The Brāhmaṇas may be termed repertoires of theological and ritual observations and comprise two elements: the prescriptive or vidhi and the explanatory or arthavāda.

With each Veda are grouped one or more Brāhmaṇas, except for the Atharvaveda which has only one. The most important of those that belong to the Rigveda is the Aitareya Brāhmaṇa; but the most formidable from the point of view of size and content is the Śatapatha Brāhmaṇa or the Brāhmaṇa of the hundred paths, made up of a hundred sections. This is grouped with the White Yajurveda and treats the rite of the new or full moon, vegetal sacrifices, the sacrifice of the soma and particularly the Agnicayana and the Agnirahasya or "mysteries of the fire (altar)".

From this Brāhmaṇa we learn that a specific sacrificial act in the soma libation requires the incantation of an appropriate mantra as well as praise of the god for whom the sacrifice is intended. The Brāhman must take constant care over the faultless performance of the ceremony which takes place in the open air before a tuft of grass. The sacrifice needs no temple and is without pomp. But behind this outward simplicity is hidden the power of the sacrificial act as it is offered to the specific god invoked or to some other personification of Brahman.

In these technical works, which may be termed manuals of Vedic orthodoxy, are found cosmogonic legends, epic tales, theomachies, anecdotes about the goddesses or, as in the

Brāhmaṇas of the Sāmaveda, commentaries on the sāmans (melodies).

The Brāhmaṇas cannot be dated. It is thought that their composition may extend over a period of some length. A considerable difference in form can be discerned between the oldest and the newest Brāhmaṇas. Taken together, their style stands out for its originality. They can certainly not be compared to any other productions of Indian literature.

THE ĀRAṆYAKAS

The Āraṇyakas or "forest treatises" are works of a somewhat esoteric nature (rahasya) which were habitually recited outside of the community in the isolation of the forests, presumably on account of the exceedingly powerful virtue of their mantras.

There are two Āraṇyakas attached to the Rigveda: the Aitareya and the Śāṅkhāyana, each of them belonging to Brāhmaṇas of the same name. They contain an account of the inner "Agnihotra" as well as mystic formulas.

From the Yajurveda we have the Taittirīya Āraṇyaka (with a commentary by Sāyaṇa) in ten prapāṭhakas. It consists of a mixture of verse (particularly about the horse sacrifice, the human sacrifice and the fire altar) and prose (on the pravargya rite and others). It follows the saṁhitās and Brāhmaṇas of the same name. One portion of it is traditionally ascribed to the Kaṭha school, which also provides us with fragments of another Āraṇyaka.

With the White Yajurveda is found the Śatapatha Brāhmaṇa which finishes in an Āraṇyaka bearing the same name as the following Upaniṣad—the Bṛhad Āraṇyaka—and this also treats of the pravargya.

The Sāmaveda contains in its saṁhitā the Āraṇyakasaṁhitā and the Āraṇyagāna. In addition we find there the beginning of the Chāndogya Upaniṣad.

THE UPANIṢADS

Coming after the Brāhmaṇas are texts containing philosophical lyricism and grandiose imagery that incorporate in a remarkable manner the principal axioms of universal metaphysics. These texts are the Upaniṣads, the compilation of which was continued actively for more than a thousand years.

Here are new growths springing up from the old, clarifying and enriching the existing Vedic works. They are still in use in Brāhman schools, collected in the form of single leaves; they constitute the last portion of the sacred books of Śruti (revelation).

The Upaniṣads give metaphoric expression to the highest anxieties of mankind, and provide answers to these in the form of treatises or of poems that are cosmic in inspiration. They are the basis of orthodox esoteric doctrine and reflect from various intellectual standpoints the pure monism that pervades them. Fairly short works generally, they continue previous lines of speculation by defining and elaborating the correspondence of ātman and Brahman, by which formula the existence of the One behind the many is sought for.

Amongst the known Upaniṣads extant, 108 represent "the essence of all Upaniṣads", but of these it is principally ten that carry the most weight. These are the Īśā, the Kena, the Kaṭha, the Muṇḍaka, the Aitareya, the Bṛhad Āraṇyaka, the Chāndogya, the Taittirīya, the Māṇḍūkya and the Praśna.

The credo of the Upaniṣads is the well-known *tat tvam asi* which can be translated "thou art that". "That" is the Absolute, i.e. Brahman, a word overwhelming in the potentialities of its meaning.

Brahman, the ritual and magic word of sacrifice in the Veda, denotes the supreme divinity. Brahman cannot be apprehended by the mind. It is transcendent, immanent, and beyond all limitation and all definition. But every being has within him a portion of Brahman: the ātman.

This ātman is impassive, immovable and eternal and is not to be confused with the ego. It is part of Brahman as is salt when it is dissolved in water:

1. "Place this salt in the water. In the morning come unto me." Then he did so.

Then he said to him: "That salt you placed in the water last evening—please, bring it hither."

Then he grasped for it, but did not find it, as it was completely dissolved.

2. "Please, take a sip of it from this end," said he. "How is it?"

"Salt."

"Take a sip from the middle," said he. "How is it?"

"Salt."

"Take a sip from that end," said he. "How is it?"

"Salt."

"Set it aside. Then come unto me."

He did so, saying, "It is always the same".

Then he said to him: "Verily, indeed, my dear, you do not perceive Being here. Verily, indeed, it is here.

3. That which is the finest essence—this whole world has that as its soul. That is Reality. That is Ātman (Soul). That art thou, Śvetaketu."

(Chānd. Up. VI. 13. i–iii.)[1]

[The Chāndogya continues:]

3. ". . . this Soul of mine within the heart is smaller than a grain of rice, or a barley corn, or a mustard seed, or a grain of millet, or the kernel of a grain of millet; this Soul of mine within the heart is greater than the earth, greater than the atmosphere, greater than the sky, greater than these worlds."

(Chānd. Up. III. 14. iii.)[2]

It is not often that metaphysics is expressed in such a poetic idiom, concrete in its imagery and drawing its beauty from the lasting freshness of nature.

By observing the visible, the Indians have discovered the invisible that is its cause, and their first philosophical notions were based on the rhythm of the Universe which they saw as identical on earth and in heaven. The heavenly bodies, the elements and the sustenance of man provide them with yardsticks. Every comparison finally is made with the sun, the moon, the corn or salt.

It is the notion only of the deity that can be adumbrated—no precision is possible, for the ātman, which is a spark from it, is defined only in negative terms. Ungraspable, it cannot be apprehended, indestructible, it cannot be destroyed; it has no

[1] Trans. Hume, *The Thirteen Principal Upanishads*, published by Oxford University Press, 1921.

[2] Trans. Hume, *ibid.*

attachments and cannot be linked to anything. It is impervious to all suffering and anxiety. This ātman is a sort of primordial unconscious and at the same time a promise of supreme bliss; the self that stands beyond human consciousness and is attained by intuitive meditation, mental concentration or yogic practice. The wise man that has discovered it knows of no more distinction between the outside world and his own personality.

20. More minute than the minute, greater than the great
Is the Soul (Ātman) that is set in the heart of a creature here,
One who is without the active will (a-kratu) beholds Him, and becomes freed from sorrow—
When through the grace (prasāda) of the Creator (dhātṛ) he beholds the greatness of the Soul (Ātman).
21. Sitting, he proceeds afar;
Lying, he goes everywhere.
Who else than I (mad) is able to know
The god (deva) who rejoices and rejoices not (madāmada)?
22. Him who is the bodiless among bodies,
Stable among the unstable,
The great, all-pervading Soul (Ātman)—
On recognizing Him, the wise man sorrows not.
23. This Soul (Ātman) is not to be obtained by instruction,
Nor by intellect, nor by much learning.
He is to be obtained only by the one whom He chooses;
To such a one that Soul (Ātman) reveals his own person (tanūm svām).

(Kaṭha Up. II. 20–23.)[3]

Pure and without blemish, no portion of Brahman absorbs either stain or defect. The Upaniṣads teach that the ātman can temporarily undergo pain or pleasure, but that it is not slain by the blow that strikes it for it inhabits the mortal body as an immortal.

When stripped of its fleshly garb, it sinks back into Brahman which is the Absolute, ākāśa, or cosmic ether. This is a sort of universal vibration in which all beings exist. It is something living rather than a space and remains ultimately untranslatable. Now this absolute which is exterior to man is the same as the

[3] Trans. Hume, *ibid.*

absolute within him. It is known as the full, as the immutable. He that knows this enjoys unending bliss. The entire basis of the Veda, of Hindu tradition or Sanātana Dharma rests upon this sacred revelation.

Since the exterior ākāśa of man is that which is also in his inmost heart, the ātman is identical with Brahman. The essence of the soul or ātman must therefore seek to be reunited with the universal essence or Brahman. The Vedic texts emphasize this tendency of the soul to return to the source that sent it forth.

> "As, from a well-blazing fire, sparks
> By the thousand issue forth of like form,
> So from the Imperishable, my friend, beings manifold
> Are produced, and thither also go."[4]
>
> (Muṇḍaka Up. II. 1. i.)

Brahman exists within the human personality just as the reflection of the sun exists in a stretch of water. The water may be disturbed or sullied, and may temporarily obscure the image which it bears but without changing its reality. Its origin prevents it from undergoing any but the most superficial changes at the hands of its surroundings. The aim of the Sanātana Dharma is attained when the ātman and the Brahman are seen as one. This is known as mokṣa or release.

When the state of the universe is expounded in some famous Upaniṣadic dialogues, an imposing poetic picture is obtained. The dialogue is in fact a frequent device in the Upaniṣads. In one of them there is a discussion between Yājñavalkya, a famous Brāhman, and Gargī, a woman philosopher who is exceptional for the esteem in which she was held. The dialogue begins by postulating the waters as the basis of the Universe for, according to the Veda, the primordial waters are the symbol of matter. Thereupon Gargī asks Yājñavalkya:

> "Yājñavalkya," said she, "since all this world is woven, warp and woof, on water, on what, pray, is the water woven, warp and woof?"
>
> "On wind, O Gargī."

[4] Trans. Hume, *ibid.*

"On what then, pray, is the wind woven, warp and woof?"

"On the atmosphere-worlds, O Gargī."

"On what then, pray, are the atmosphere-worlds woven, warp and woof?"

"On the worlds of the Gandharvas, O Gargī."

"On what then, pray, are the worlds of the Gandharvas woven, warp and woof?"

"On the worlds of the sun, O Gargī."

"On what then, pray, are the worlds of the sun woven, warp and woof?"

"On the worlds of the moon, O Gargī."

"On what then, pray, are the worlds of the moon woven, warp and woof?"

"On the worlds of the stars, O Gargī."

"On what then, pray, are the worlds of the stars woven, warp and woof?"

"On the worlds of the gods, O Gargī."

"On what then, pray, are the worlds of the gods woven, warp and woof?"

"On the worlds of Indra, O Gargī."

"On what then, pray, are the worlds of Indra woven, warp and woof?"

"On the worlds of Prajāpati, O Gargī."

"On what then, pray, are the worlds of Prajāpati woven, warp and woof?"

"On the worlds of Brahma, O Gargī."

"On what then, pray, are the worlds of Brahma woven, warp and woof?"

Yājñavalkya said: "Gargī, do not question too much, lest your head fall off. In truth you are questioning too much about a divinity about which further questions cannot be asked. Gargī, do not over-question."

Thereupon Gargī Vācaknavī held her peace.

(Bṛ. Ar. Up. III. 6.)[5]

Among the most important Upaniṣads, the Īśā Upaniṣad still remains to be mentioned. It is so called after the word with which it begins. Perhaps the first of the verse Upaniṣads, it stands at the head of the whole collection, and belongs to one of the saṁhitās of the Yajurveda.

This short poem postulates the principle of a sovereign who

[5] Trans. Hume, *ibid.*

encompasses the Universe and it declares that above all it is the Self or ātman that should be known as the universal Self or Brahman. For the man capable of realizing this transcendence all barriers fall and he is freed from becoming and non-becoming.

1. By the Lord (īśā) enveloped must all this be—
Whatever moving thing there is in the moving world.
With this renounced, thou mayest enjoy.
Covet not the wealth of anyone at all.
3. Devilish (asurya) are those worlds called,
With blind darkness (tamas) covered o'er!
Unto them, on deceasing, go
Whatever folk are slayers of the Self.
7. In whom all beings
Have become just (eva) the Self of the discerner—
Then what delusion (moha), what sorrow (śoka) is there,
Of him who perceives the unity!
10. (The ātman-Brahman is) other, indeed, they say, than knowledge!
Other, they say, than non-knowledge!
—Thus we have heard from the wise (dhīra)
Who to us have explained It.
17. [My] breath (vāyu) to the immortal wind (anila)!
This body then ends in ashes! Om!
O Purpose (kratu), remember! The deed (kṛta) remember!
O Purpose, remember! The deed remember!

(Iś. Up. 1, 3, 7, 10, 17.)

The first verse of the Īśā Upaniṣad was added by Mahātma Gandhi to his first daily prayer in the following form:

"All that exists in this world is subject to change; wrap all your perceptions in the divine; it is by this renunciation that you shall become (spiritually) enriched; do not covet the portion of whomsoever it may be (for nothing belongs to you)."

In the Kena Upaniṣad the analysis of consciousness is the central theme which teaches how this consciousness may be revealed in the very depths of one's being. This Upaniṣad belongs to the Sāmaveda. It asks who has created the phenomenal world and alludes to the unfathomable mystery that lies behind it, and which none can understand.

"It is conceived of by him by whom it is not conceived of.
He by whom it is not conceived of, knows it not.
It is not understood by those who [say they] understand it.
It is understood by those who [say they] understand it not."
(Kena Up. II. 3.)[6]

The Muṇḍaka Upaniṣad belongs to the Atharvaveda and it has been considered as one of the sources of the Bhagavad Gītā.

This Upaniṣad, which is written in verse, admits the value of ritualism, but prefers to stress knowledge of Brahman through knowledge of Puruṣa (the cosmic form of Brahman), and knowledge of the ātman (the individual form of Brahman). In this way will the cycle of rebirths be ended. The Muṇḍaka Upaniṣad is later than the Chāndogya.

4. Fire is his head; his eyes, the moon and sun;
The regions of space, his ears; his voice the revealed Vedas;
Wind, his breath (prāṇa); his heart, the whole world. Out of his feet,
The earth. Truly, he is the Inner Soul (Ātman) of all.
(Muṇḍ. Up. II. 1. iv.)

4. The mystic syllable Om (praṇava) is the bow. The arrow is the soul (ātman).
Brahma is said to be the mark (lakṣya).
By the undistracted man is it to be penetrated.
One should come to be in it, as the arrow [in the mark].
(Muṇḍ. Up. II. 2. iv.)

3. When a seer sees the brilliant
Maker, Lord, Person, the Brahma-source,
Then, being a knower, shaking off good and evil,
Stainless, he attains supreme identity (sāmya) [with him].
(Muṇḍ. Up. III. 1. iii.)[7]

The Māṇḍūkya Upaniṣad has inspired one of the most original works of Indian philosophy: the Kārikās of Gauḍapāda (possibly 7th cent.). As an absolute monist, Gauḍapāda is one of the masters of the Vedānta.

"As when the jars are broken the space they contained becomes one again with all space, so is the relation of jīvas to the ātman".
(Gauḍapāda, Kārikā, iii).

[6] Trans. Hume, *ibid.*
[7] Trans. Hume, *ibid.*

CHAPTER IV

SMṚTI

THE PURĀṆAS

Tradition, which regards the Purāṇas or "Antiquities" as sacred books, sometimes even ranks them with the Vedas and attributes them collectively to Vyāsa, the mythical author of the Mahābhārata. Their language is simple and without literary pretension and they are held to be especially suitable for women and Śūdras.

Since they teach religious practices and ritual, these texts are counted among the most important. Knowledge of the Purāṇas is indispensable for an understanding of the religions of India. In them can be found cosmogonic legends from the Prajāpati cycle, numerous discussions, tales of pilgrimage and descriptions of sacred places. Some give accounts of royal dynasties. All of Hindu mythology is expressed in the Purāṇas. Taken as a whole, their purpose is primarily religious. The capital notion of the sacrifice, which is already present in the Rigveda, forms the basis of their doctrine and this is expounded together with discussions on the nature of the life-breath and on phonetics.

Though far too little known by the mass of the wider public, the Purāṇas represent an important source, going back to the most ancient times, for Hindu religious history.

The major Purāṇas, numbering eighteen in all, are dedicated to Viṣṇu, Śiva and Brahman. One of the most famous is that which tells of the life of Kṛṣṇa; another, the seventh, is devoted to the journey to hell of king Vipaścit. In date they extend from the first centuries of the Christian era until the twelfth.

MĀRKAṆḌEYA PURĀṆA

In the middle of a description of hell in the Mārkaṇḍeya occurs the following moving legend, told in the rough and concise language of the ancient tales. King Vipaścit has been taken down to hell by a servant of the King of the Dead, Yama, for, though his conduct had been exemplary all his life, yet for a trifling error of inattention he has incurred an instant's punishment. The servant shows him beings condemned to torture and then invites him to leave this unhappy place. Hereupon follows the miracle. . . .

The King said:

"Ho! servant of Yama! say, what sin have I committed, for which I have incurred this deepest hell, frightful for its torments? Known as Vipaścit, I was born in the family of the Janakas, in the country of Videha, in very truth a guardian of men. I sacrificed with many sacrifices; I protected the earth with uprightness; nor did I let fighting rage; no guest departed with averted countenance; nor did I offend the pitṛs, the gods, the ṛṣis or my servants; nor did I covet other men's wives, or wealth, or aught else belonging to them. At the moon's changes the pitṛs, on other lunar days the gods, voluntarily approached mankind as cows a pool. The two religious duties, both sacrifice and meritorious work, perish inasmuch as the performers of domestic sacrifices depart sighing with averted faces. The merit amassed in seven lives is dissipated by the sighing of the pitṛs; the sighing assuredly destroys the destiny that springs from three lives. Hence I was ever indeed kindly disposed to what concerned the gods and the pitṛs; being such, how have I incurred this very terrible hell?"

Yama's servant spoke:

"Come then, we go elsewhere. Thou hast now seen everything, for thou hast seen hell. Come then, let us go elsewhere."

The reciter spoke:

"Thereupon the king prepared to follow him; and then a cry went up from all the men that abode in torment, 'Be gracious, O king! stay but a moment, for the air that clings to thy body gladdens our mind, and entirely dispels the burning and the sufferings and pains from our bodies, O tiger-like man! Be gracious, O king!'

"On hearing this their entreaty, the king asked that servant of Yama, 'How do I afford gladness to these men? Have I done such a mighty deed of merit in the world of mortals, wherefrom falls this gladdening shower? Declare me that.' "

Yama's servant spoke:

"Inasmuch as thy body was nourished with the food that remained, after the pitṛs, the gods, guests and servants were satisfied, and since thy mind was attached to them, hence the air that clings to thy body brings gladness; the torment, O king! does not hurt the evil-doers. Whereas thou didst offer the horse-sacrifice and other sacrifices according to precept, hence from seeing thee Yama's engines, weapons, fires and crows, which cause intense suffering, such as crushing, cutting, burning and so forth, grow mild, O king! when counteracted by majesty."

The king spoke:

"Neither in Svarga nor in Brahma-loka do men experience such joy, methinks, as arises from conferring bliss on suffering creatures. If, while I am present, torment does not hurt these men, here then, fair Sir, I will remain firm as a mountain."

Yama's servant spoke:

"Come, O king; we proceed. Enjoy the delights won by thine own merit, casting aside here the torments of evil-doers."

The king spoke:

"For that reason I will not go as long as these are in sore suffering. From my near-presence the denizens of hell grow happy. Fie on the sickly protection-begging life of that man who shews no favour to one distressed, even though he be a resolute foe! Sacrifices, gifts, austerities do not work for the welfare of him who has no thought for the succour of the distressed. Whoever bears a cruel mind towards children, the sick and such like, and towards the aged also, I do not hold him human; he is truly a Rākṣasa. But if these men have pain originating in hell, whether produced by the heat from fire or produced by overpowering smells, and if they have the intense pain arising from hunger and thirst that causes faintness, yet the grant of deliverance to them excels, I consider, the joy of Svarga. If many sufferers shall obtain happiness, while I undergo pain, should I not in truth embrace it? Go thou not therefore long".

Yama's servant spoke:

"Here have both Dharma and Indra arrived to lead thee away. Thou must certainly depart from us: go therefore, O king!"

Dharma spoke:

"Fittingly worshipped by thee, I lead thee to Svarga; mount this heavenly chariot and linger not; let us go."

The king spoke:

"Men in thousands, O Dharma! suffer pain here in hell; and being in affliction they cry to me to save them; hence I depart not."

Indra spoke:

"These evil-doers have come to hell in consequence of their own deeds; thou also, O king, must go to Svarga in consequence of thy meritorious deed."

The king spoke:

"If thou dost know, thou, O Dharma, or thou, O Indra, Śacī's lord, how great indeed is my authority, then deign to speak aright."

Dharma spoke:

"Just as drops of water in the sea, or as stars in the sky, or as showers of rain, as the sands in the Ganges—just as these drops of water and other things are innumerable, O mahā-rājā! even so thy merit is in truth beyond reckoning. In thy evincing now this compassion here in the hells, the reckoning of that merit of thine has verily amounted to a hundred thousand. Then go, O king! enjoy then the abode of the immortals; let these also consume away in hell the sin arising from their own actions."

The king spoke:

"How shall men attain their desire in things connected with me, if in my presence these people gain no prosperity? Hence, whatever good deeds I possess, O lord of the thirty gods! by means thereof let the sinners who are undergoing torment be delivered from hell!"

Indra spoke:

"Thus hast thou, O king! gained a more exalted station; see too these sinners delivered from hell!"

The reciter spoke:

"Then fell there a shower of flowers upon that king, and Hari making him mount the heavenly chariot led him to the heaven-world."[8]

[8] Trans. Pargiter, *Mārkaṇḍeya Purāṇa*, Bib. Ind. 125, pp. 75, 88–91.

THE TANTRAS

As in the case of the Purāṇas, the Tantras are "books" which can be divided into Vaiṣṇavite treatises called Saṁhitās and Śaivite treatises called Āgamas and lastly the Tantras belonging to the religious phenomenon known as Tantrism.

THE SŪTRAS

The Vedic Sūtras which are part of Smṛti are considered to be technical works of scholastic instruction. They are composed in a highly concise style consisting of aphorisms (sūtras) and contain the views or darśanas of certain of the schools towards secular and administrative law. They are both religious and secular. Some of them deal with astronomy, prosody or phonetics.

THE LAWS OF MANU

The Laws of Manu or the Mānavadharmaśāstra, composed around the beginning of the Christian era, are among the best known of the texts. They describe Indian society, caste, the rules of the domestic cult and the order of the solemn ceremonies. In addition there are considerable philosophic speculations on the destiny of the soul, on the consequences of action and on salvation. The totality of all these quite important texts forms what is known as the Dharmaśāstra or Instruction on the Law and is a sort of theoretical and idealistic code of the Hindu tradition.

THE GREAT EPICS

The Bhagavadgītā

The great epic cycle, which plays an important part in Indian history and literature and revives the grandiose poetry already found in the Vedic hymns, occupies the first place amongst the oldest of the post-Vedic literary documents.

It began to be compiled in the second century or even earlier in the case of some episodes. It is composed in Sanskrit but, properly speaking, is not a religious work, though entirely impregnated with a fervent mysticism.

It consists of long tales of adventure inspired from ancient legends that would seem sometimes to contain historical elements. This is particularly true wherever allusion is made to specific wars and also because the royal heroes of the Bharata tribe "are the immediate ancestors of king Janameya, the son of Parikṣit, of whom the later Vedic texts speak as a contemporary and before whom the Epic is said to have been recited for the first time" (Renou).

This vast collection takes the form of two epic poems (itihāsas): the Mahābhārata and the Rāmāyaṇa which can justly claim a place in world literature. Few works can have provoked as much enthusiasm as the former when it was published in 1785 in a translation by Wilkins. Its authorship is traditionally attributed to Vyāsa. The core of the first poem, which is the longer of the two, is called the Bhagavadgītā. It describes the struggle between two branches of the same family: on the one side the five Pāṇḍava brothers, amongst whom is Arjuna, and on the other their uncle Dhṛtarāṣṭra with Duryodhana and his ninety-nine brothers, the Kauravas.

The Bhagavadgītā is only a fragment of the Mahābhārata, which in all contains 100,000 couplets. It is a mixture of religious and warlike legends with philosophical concepts and from it has shone a light that is still far from extinction.

The Bhagavadgītā is filled with religious fervour. Its theme is that of Bhakti or complete union with the sole Being, whose name may change and whose names are innumerable. This Being becomes incarnate as Kṛṣṇa, identified in the poem with the universal Soul, in order to pour out the treasures of his thought on Arjuna who listens before giving battle.

Two speculative systems, monism and dualism, are introduced in turn. The Gītā does not, however, adopt any particular doctrine with fixed and rigid dogmas within an orthodox framework but rather does it represent a religious orientation which was passionately adopted and retained within the Hindu tradition.

Arjuna, one of the Pāṇḍavas, is stricken with anguish on the eve of battle (a dreadful battle is about to take place which will rage for eighteen days. The earth will be covered with the dead and the dying and the sky will be darkened by arrows). He broods on the death that will strike perhaps even the best, those whom he loves and who are even now drawn up in battle array. But Kṛṣṇa condemns the thoughts of Arjuna "that lead neither to heaven nor to honour".

He teaches him that once a man has been born it is for all time and that he cannot die:

> 12. Never have I not been, never hast thou and never have these princes of men not been: and never shall time yet come when we shall not all be.
>
> 13. As the Body's Tenant goes through childhood and manhood and old age in this body, so does it pass to other bodies; the wise man is not confounded therein. (Bhagavadgītā, II).

The impressions of the wise are fugitive and have but to be borne, for "he that is not disquieted by these, that remains steady in pain and pleasure . . . fitly prepares himself for eternal life."

Kṛṣṇa expounds the Vedic religion and the indestructibility of the frame of the Universe. He declares it to be imperishable:

> 18. It is these bodies of the everlasting, unperishing, incomprehensible Body-Dweller that have an end, as it is said, therefore fight, O thou of Bharata's race.
>
> 20. This never is born, and never dies, nor may it after being come again to be not; this unborn, everlasting, abiding Ancient is not slain when the body is slain.
>
> 22. As a man lays aside outworn garments and takes others that are new, so the Body-Dweller puts away outworn bodies and goes to others that are new.
>
> 23. Weapons cleave not This, fire burns not This, waters wet not This, wind dries it not.
>
> 25. Unshown is This called, unthinkable This, unalterable This; therefore, knowing it in this wise, thou dost not well to grieve.
>
> (Bhagavadgītā, II.)

Therefore Kṛṣṇa offers Arjuna the sensible consolation that there is no room for sorrow for that which has to be. Hence, even if Arjuna thinks that the soul is born or dies, he must remember this: "28. Born beings have for their beginning the unshown state, for their midway the shown, O thou of Bharata's race, and for their ending the unshown; what lament is there for this?" (Bhagavadgītā, II.)

The Kṛṣṇa reminds Arjuna that nothing should take precedence over his caste-duty as a kṣatriya and that his obligation is to accomplish this without being weakened by pity. (Here we are far from Buddhism and the principle of non-action.) Kṛṣṇa continues: "34. Also born beings will tell of thee a tale of unchanging dishonour; and to a man of repute dishonour is more than death. 38. Holding in indifference alike pleasure and pain, gain and loss, conquest and defeat, so make thyself ready for the fight; thus shalt thou get no sin" (Bhagavadgītā, II).

And after inspiring him with a valour worthy of his caste, Kṛṣṇa prepares Arjuna for a higher stoicism. His purest advice, in which he is a predecessor of Kant, is: "47. In Works be thine office; in their fruits must it never be. Be not moved by the fruits of Works; but let not attachment to worklessness dwell in thee" (Bhagavadgītā, II).

If the 100,000 couplets of the Mahābhārata had contained in their sands only the jewel that is the Bhagavadgītā, this thought alone would have sufficed to ensure their glory.

To be unmoved before success or failure, to be devoid of all attachments and to discover in meditation the sole refuge after having acted in accordance with one's conscience; this is the summary of the course of action that Kṛṣṇa exalts when he disparages those that "have the fruit of action as their motive".

There is great grandeur in accomplishing one's duty and in acquitting oneself of obligations without any thought of a possible reward in heaven or on earth. But action, even though it be the link that holds the world together, does not suffice to lead one to salvation, since "for the man whose delight is in Self, who is contented with Self, and is glad of Self, there is naught for which he should work". (Bhagavadgītā, III. 17).

The truth is masked by that eternal enemy of the wise man, the insatiable fire that is desire:

> 41. Therefore do thou first by constraint of the sense-instruments, O Bharata-prince, loose thyself from this sinful one that destroys knowledge and discernment.
>
> 42. The sense-instruments, they say, are high; higher than the sense-instruments is the mind; higher than the mind is understanding; but higher than understanding is This.
>
> 43. Thus, knowing Self to be higher than understanding, and supporting by Self thyself, O mighty-armed one, slay this changeling foe so hard to reach.
>
> (Bhagavadgītā, III.)

Kṛṣṇa, the god of the universal Soul, defines himself thus to Arjuna:

> 6. Though birthless and unchanging of essence, and though lord of born beings, yet in my sway over the Nature that is mine own I come into birth by my own Magic.
>
> 7. For whensoever the Law fails and lawlessness uprises, O thou of Bharata's race, then do I bring myself to bodied birth.
>
> 9. He who knows in verity my divine birth and works comes not again to birth when he has left the body; he comes to me, O Arjuna.
>
> 10. Many, freed from passion, fear and wrath, instinct with me, making their home in me, and cleansed by the mortifications of knowledge, have come into my Being.
>
> 11. With them that seek me I deal in like measure. [. . .]
>
> (Bhagavadgītā, IV.)

Though indifferent to action and the fruits of action, Kṛṣṇa recommends the sacrifice that was the first concept of the Vedic religion. But the Gītā teaches that "there is more bliss in sacrifice of knowledge than in sacrifice of substance . . .; all Works without limit . . . are contained in knowledge" (Bhagavadgītā, IV. 33).

36. "Even though thou shouldst be of all sinners the greatest evildoer, thou shalt be by the boat of knowledge carried over all evil" (Bhagavadgītā, IV).

Amongst those passages where devotion to Kṛṣṇa is particularly in evidence we find this these further statements: 30. "If one sees me in all things and all things in me, I am not lost to him, nor is he lost to me" (Bhagavadgītā, VI).

5. "He who at his last hour, when he casts off the body, goes hence remembering me, goes assuredly into my being."

(Bhagavadgītā, VIII.)[9]

Two long romantic episodes in the Mahābhārata are also worthy of mention as being of real literary value. These are the Tale of Nala and Damayantī and the poem of Savitrī, the pure and virtuous princess. Both are episodes of great beauty.

If the Mahābhārata has been rightly considered the summation of Hinduism—and it has been called the fifth Veda—then the Bhagavadgītā bears the dignity of a sort of Gospel (Renou). Hence it is held by way of exception as part of Śruti.

The Rāmāyaṇa

The Rāmāyaṇa, the other epic poem in the great cycle, is much shorter than the Mahābhārata. It consists of only 640 sargas or cantos. Hindu tradition attributes it to a single author, Vālmīki, who is considered a seer after the fashion of the ṛṣis. He is supposed to have "seen" the Rāmāyaṇa and tradition regards him as having himself taken part in some of its events. Another most attractive legend claims that Vālmīki ended by being an ascetic who remained a thousand years so motionless that his body was covered by an anthill (valmīka)—hence his name: son of the anthill (Renou).

This epic traces the life of the hero Rāma (an incarnation of Viṣṇu), the eldest son of king Daśaratha, to whom Sītā, daughter of king Janaka, was given in marriage. After years of happiness, Sītā is kidnapped by a demon. Rāma goes off to find and rescue her. The poem is an account of the exploits that Rāma has to accomplish to recover Sītā, who is the symbol of purity and fidelity, and of the trials she has to undergo on her part. A succession of different episodes, warlike, poetic and moving, takes place in an atmosphere that is sometimes luxurious and

[9] Trans. L. D. Barnett, *Bhagavadgītā* (1905), published by J. M. Dent & Sons, London.

sometimes pastoral but always religious and instinct with the sense of duty. The end is pathetic. Rāma repudiates Sītā and she, to attest her purity, invokes the Earth "to admit her if she has not lied". The Earth opens up and admits Sītā into her depths. Sītā is one of the most touching figures in the epic cycle. In vain Rāma begs that she might be restored to him. After a time he himself ascends to heaven to resume his shape as Viṣṇu.

The Rāmāyaṇa and the Mahābhārata have become widespread like no other work in Indian literature.

CHAPTER V

THE PHILOSOPHICAL SYSTEMS OR DARŚANAS

In the Hindu tradition religion and philosophy are but two inseparable aspects of the same thing. However unfettered speculation may be, the various metaphysical and cosmological conceptions of India do not constitute different doctrines but are rather to be thought of as developments of certain "points of view" of the same doctrine and, though they tend in various directions, they are far from being mutually incompatible. The Sanskrit word "darśana" carries exactly this meaning of "point of view". It denotes each of the conceptions that have sprung from their common origin in the Vedas. The darśanas throw light on, and complement, each other. They might be compared to the branches of a tree, all growing in different directions but belonging still to the same tree. In Indian religion it is agreement with the Vedas which is the criterion of orthodoxy.

The founders of these darśanas—or philosophical systems—were great saints and great mystics. Their constant aim was to return to purer forms of religion and to maintain the authentic tradition.

These darśanas, systems or schools are six in number and constitute a complete picture of the Universe. As successors to the Brāhmaṇas and the Upaniṣads, they teach the knowledge that leads to cognition and liberation. For a knowledge of Indian culture a study of the darśanas is indispensable.

The darśanas were already in existence in Vedic times but it was during the Vedāntic period that they were developed and formulated. The systems that go under the name of darśana are most varied. The Buddhist doctrines or the theories of the materialists are held to be darśanas. This is the case with the materialism of Cārvāka which has become a darśana bearing the name of its founder. In this system everything is brought back to sensation. Inference, induction and causality are denied. There is no reality outside that of the four elements—earth, air, fire and water. These principles combine variously to produce all matter. Even thought is but the result of such a union. The soul and the body are identical.

The basic text of the Cārvākas, attributed to Bṛhaspati, was written i n the form of sūtras but it is the Sarvadarśanasaṁgraha of Mādhava (fourteenth century) that gives the most complete exposition of the materialist system. (Renou, *L'Inde classique*, II, p. 74.)

The term darśana is especially applied to the six Brāhmanic darśanas which recognize the paramount authority of the Vedas, the Brāhmaṇas and the Upaniṣads. The sum of their various views constitutes a total picture of the Universe.

The study of the darśanas in the Hindu schools begins with the Nyāya-Vaiśeṣika, continues through the Sāṁkhya-Yoga and finishes with the Mīmāṁsā and the Vedānta. Thus the student advances step by step from the most direct knowledge to the understanding of the Absolute.

THE FIRST DARŚANA: THE VAIŚEṢIKA

Although very ancient, the Vaiśeṣika was not constituted into a system till the composition of the sūtras on it. The aim of this darśana is to bring an end to the sorrow of human kind by making available to it the direct vision, that is, by making it fulfil its Self.

Spiritual and material substances are distinguished. The system describes and delimits in their particularities the elements of Nature or prakṛti. It may be thought of as a kind of physical science. It is related to the Nyāya darśana.

In the Vaiśeṣika system material bodies are composed of infinitely small atoms which are eternal and indestructible and impelled by an invisible force. They combine according to specific laws to form binary, tertiary and quaternary molecules in building up material bodies. Joined to those atomic combinations are multiple and countless ātmans involved in the phenomenal world and consequently in the wheel of rebirth. The atoms exist in a continuum called ākāśa or spatial ether. An atom is defined as being "comparable in size with the sixth part of a speck of dust visible in a ray of sunlight." (Renou, *op. cit.*, p. 73.) Every ātman that is combined with a manas, through which it observes the universe, becomes closely associated with it. The cause of the determinism that impels it into transmigration is due to this union of mind with matter.

By discovering its real nature the ātman becomes free. Thus it breaks the bond of saṁsāra.

The Vaiśeṣika writers describe nine substances as composing the universe: earth (pṛthivī), water (āpas), fire (tejas), air (vāyu), ether (ākāśa), time (kāla), direction in space (diś), soul (ātman) and understanding (manas). The guṇas are the qualities of these substances. They characterize them in their activities and in their properties. It must be noted that the ether is not atomic but the medium of the transmission of sound. "It is the divine will and karma which, according to some Vaiśeṣika authors, in turn combine and separate the atoms in order to create and destroy the universe." (Renou, *op. cit.*, p. 73.) The Vaiśeṣika writers define dharma as being the means by which one may arrive at the highest stage of development. The practical contribution of this darśana to the goal of salvation is that it leads to a training of the mind based upon a methodical classification of values. A capital distinction is made between the manas "mind" or "understanding" and the soul. Unlike the ātman, the manas is not universal but atomic. Whereas the ātman embraces the whole world, the manas, however spiritual, remains tied to the level of the sentient being. The Vaiśeṣikasūtras are attributed to Kaṇāda.

The central point of this darśana concerns the ātman. Evidence for its existence lies in every biological and psychological phenomenon. "The rhythm of life, the movement of the spirit, sensations, sentiments and volitions are all of them proof of the existence of the ātman. The oldest Vaiśeṣika work after the Sūtras seems to be the Padārthadharmasaṁgraha of Praśastapāda" (Grousset, *Philosophies indiennes*, II, p. 74).

THE SECOND DARŚANA: THE NYĀYA

The word Nyāya originally meant "logic". The Nyāya system is a darśana attributed to Akṣapāda Gautama and its principal study is that of logic taken in a somewhat less limited sense than in the West. This logic is held to be a "point of view" of the total doctrine and this extends its application.

The Nyāya can further be described as an "inquiry of the spirit", a method of knowledge in which things are considered as "objects of proof" and classed into categories.

The Nyāyasūtras, the fundamental text of the Nyāya system, distinguish sixteen elements or padārthas in the operations of the mind. The first is called pramāṇa and means "proof" or criterion. The second is called prameya and indicates that which is to be measured, i.e. the measurable. As a subdivision of it is found a classification of all the things that can be attained by human understanding.

The Nyāya, which is combined with the Vaiśeṣika, the sūtras of which are older, employs a kind of syllogism as its particular form of reasoning. This reasoning can also be applied to the spiritual domain and can lead to Release which, according to the Hindus, is attained through correct knowledge.

The first sūtra proclaims that the "knowledge of the sixteen elements of dialectic permits one to reach the supreme good". By a connected sequence of logical steps the conclusion reached in the Nyāyasūtras is that the sorrow of existence is caused by ignorance and false knowledge. "The Nyāya teaches one to think correctly concerning the phenomena whose existence it acknowledges. In this respect it is an indispensable instrument for a science that uses it to prove its theories. This is why it is used in medicine and was described by Caraka" (L. Renou, *op. cit.*, p. 56).

The Nyāya recognizes the existence of a supreme god: Īśvara. But its aim is not theology. "The theism of the Nyāya assumed a particular importance in the tenth century in the works of its commentator Udayana, works which Barth has called one of the most religious products of Sanskrit literature. Nonetheless it is true that, as a system of logic, the Nyāya is acceptable to anyone, regardless of his creed" (L. Renou, *ibid*).

THE THIRD DARŚANA: THE SĀṀKHYA

The Sāṁkhya, one of the most elaborate systems of Indian philosophy, is a darśana whose task it is to enumerate and analyse the elements of nature or the universal manifestation, in order to synthesize them. The name Sāṁkhya means "that which derives from number" which is an allusion to the characteristic use of enumerations and classifications in this darśana. It is Kapila, the great sage of yore, who is the author of the Sāṁkhyasūtras.

The Sāṁkhya system is dualist and recognizes two planes: that of the phenomenal, of prakṛti and of universal nature, and that of the transcendental—of puruṣa, the spirit.

Prakṛti, with the three guṇas or modalities that qualify it, forms the totality of all phenomena. It encompasses simultaneously all the phenomena themselves and also their perception by man, that is, the physical and psychical worlds.

Ruled by a determinism expressed in remarkable scientific formulas, prakṛti evolves from the indistinct and subtle state to the gross state, that is, from the homogeneous to the heterogeneous.

Unlike nature, the spirit (puruṣa) or the particular ātmans are impersonal and neuter. The union of puruṣa and prakṛti creates the universe, for prakṛti, primordially inert, begins to act only when set in motion by puruṣa, thereby producing living entities. And thus also is created universal sorrow. By uniting with puruṣa, prakṛti imprisons the purely noumenal and impassive monad and turns it into a jīva, a living and suffering personality, to which life gives karma and which is plunged by karma into the indefinite round of saṁsāra and the sorrow of existence. Release (mokṣa) means the liberation of the puruṣa, the noumenal soul, from the bonds of prakṛti.

Characteristic of the Sāṁkhya is its hierarchic enumeration of different stages of being in a state of manifestation. This system is comprised in twenty-five tattvas or "principles" and "elements" corresponding to these hierarchized stages and maintains throughout that puruṣa and prakṛti exist for all eternity.

Prakṛti then is our starting-point. As the universal substrate of all phenomena, capable of indefinite activity, it constitutes the efficient and material cause of the world and is at the same time held to be a substance in the same way as its derivatives. Though absolutely one, it is yet composed of three essences—the guṇas (Renou). Prakṛti is the undetermined (avyakta), the pre-established principle (pradhāna). The guṇas enter into prakṛti both as inherent parts and as qualities of it—qualities when in relation to it, prakṛti, though substances when taken by themselves.

As with all the constructs of the Sāṁkhya system, the guṇas must be seen as both physical (macrocosmic) and psychical (microcosmic) elements. The noblest of them, sattva, corresponds to physical and spiritual light. The second, rajas, is energy, passion, that which sets in train, both in nature and in man, actions and sufferings. Tamas (darkness) is the weight, the obstacle, that which maintains the inorganic world in its passivity, blinding and misleading mankind. Sattva and tamas are by themselves inactive; it is rajas that provides the motive power. Whatever guṇa is predominant in a given object imparts to it the qualities entailed thereby. The pleasure we derive from flowers is due to the sattva inherent in them.

In the inert state of nature, in mūlaprakṛti or "primordial nature", the guṇas are in equilibrium. It is the stage of avyakta, of the unevolved, or, in cosmogonic terms, the stage of pralaya, "dissolution". But at a given moment this balance is broken; progressing by itself, with no exterior aid, or, as is also said, impelled by the proximity of puruṣa, which affects it as might a magnet, prakṛti sets in motion the mechanism of evolution. (Renou, *op. cit.*, pp. 38, 39.)

The Sāṁkhya is an evolutionary explanation of the universe, the aim of which is release. It is this explanation that is used by the Yoga system to attain its goal of physiological and psychological mastery, for the Sāṁkhya and Yoga systems complement each other as do the Vaiśeṣika and Nyāya, since they too analyse spirit and matter.

THE FOURTH DARŚANA: THE YOGA

The word Yoga means "union" in Sanskrit and it designates principally the effective union of the human being with the universal, which is achieved by following certain age-old precepts.

The term Yoga is also applied to a darśana. Its formulation into sūtras is attributed to Patañjali. The Yoga of Patañjali, which is a specific ascesis, knows of a personal god, Īśvara.

The Yogasūtras teach him who so wishes to become "what he is", that is, to realize within himself the puruṣa that is his true essence. To attain this end, a double discipline is necessary. First of all, the destruction of the sense of personal identity, or bringing into an abeyance as totally as possible the operations of one's own mind, and secondly, the immersion of the spirit into the inner noumen.

The Yoga system represents from the practical point of view the realization of the Sāṁkhya, of which it is indeed the complementary darśana. It uses elements defined by the other darśanas in order to gain a mastery that is both psychological and physiological. "The fire of Yoga burns the cage of sin that surrounds man. Knowledge becomes pure and Nirvāṇa is directly obtained. From Yoga comes awareness, and awareness in its turn helps the Yogin. He that combines in himself both Yoga and knowledge pleases the Supreme Lord."

The concept of Yoga traditionally means the following:

1. Yoga brings about the union of the finite (jīvātman) with the infinite (parātman).
2. Yoga depends on a mental energy that disciplines the mind (manas).

3. It is, according to the description frequently found in the Upaniṣads, the total fusion of the individual with the universal.

4. Yoga is the completely pure state (sāttvik) in which man, freed from ignorance (avidyā), may attain the highest spiritual fulfilment.

"Yoga prepares the way which leads to spiritual enlightenment and ultimately to salvation. This is, Yoga undertakes to give to the spirit the supreme good, whereby material obstacles become auxiliaries to such an extent that Nature herself is shorn of her light and retires beaten from the field."

(Usha Chatterji, *Comprendre la religion hindoue*, p. 88.)

The Yogin must learn to consider all things in their true light, for only truth will permit him to attain the Supreme (parātman),

The first step on this path is the suppression of earthly desires and appetites. To break the continuity of the chain of life, the help of Yoga must be sought. The Yogin must not hope to know a better form of life after death, such as becoming a god or a pure spirit. On this point the Yoga systems of Buddhism, Jainism and Hinduism are agreed. The transitory phenomenal world must disappear step by step. Then the ātman can come into real contact with the parātman.

Having reached this state, the Yogin experiences a sensation of complete detachment which is known as paravairāgya. Only then does a clear apprehension of the ātman become possible.

The obstacles that are held to beset the path of a Yogin are:

1. Illness. Yoga can certainly help to maintain the body in perfect health, but to take the first steps on the path of Yoga good health is necessary. Yoga gives to its adepts an hypersensitivity, an astounding control over the body and the mind, even to the extent of voluntarily inflicting death upon oneself. But all this must be devoted to a single end: union with the Absolute. These powers lose all meaning and disappear quickly when they are used for purposes of personal vainglory. They become instruments that cannot find within themselves their own justification.

2. Laziness. Of the three states of mind that exist, the Yogin

must banish two, the rājasik and tāmasik states, in order to fix himself into the sāttvik state which alone can lead him into the true path of Yoga.

3. Doubt. The Yogin must not doubt himself or the value of his quest. Without an absolute belief in the supreme truth, he cannot encompass his new life. It would all appear far too difficult to him.

4. Lack of concentration. The spirit must concentrate on a single thought—spiritual perfection. All other considerations must go.

5. Egoism and excessive attachment to the world. The Yogin must convince himself from the beginning that the phenomenal world is illusory and transient and that, if he wishes to attain the highest spirituality and release, he must rid himself of the false conception of the ordinary world.

It is after having overcome these obstacles that the Yogin will reach the conclusion that nothing binds the ātman to the material world under its various aspects. When he has understood, moreover, that these chains and links are but mere inventions of the human mind, he will have regained the original state of purity that will allow him to enter into contact with the divine and ultimately to fuse with it.

THE FIFTH DARŚANA: THE MĪMĀṀSĀ

The term mīmāṁsā means "investigation" or "profound reflection" and appears in all Indian literature from the Atharva- and Yajurvedas onwards. The objective of this darśana is to study the sacred texts and to determine the precise meaning of certain passages of ritual and speculation.

The Mīmāṁsā may investigate either the law or Brahman and this explains the two forms of the Mīmāṁsā. The first and more important one concerns the study of rites. It is called the Pūrvamīmāṁsā. The second is the Uttaramīmāṁsā or Vedāntamīmāṁsā. The two are at the same time contrasting and complementary.

The aim of the Sūtras of Jaimini, the oldest Mīmāṁsā treatise, was both theoretical and practical. Their task was to examine the verses (mantras) and the brāhmaṇas (interpretations) in order to establish general rules for the flawless execution of ritual.

The Mīmāṁsāsūtras are divided into twelve adhyāyas containing 2,700 sūtras. Each adhyāya is subdivided into pādas or "quarters", four in number, which deal with differing subjects (adhikaraṇa).

Dharma is the basic subject *par excellence* for the Mīmāṁsā. Later the notion of a Supreme Being assumes greater importance,

The method of presentation in the Mīmāṁsā consists of "five moments": the question is introduced for treatment (viṣaya); the doubt it brings is expressed (saṁśaya or viṣaya); a possible preliminary opinion is arrived at (uttarapakṣa) and this generally accords with the definitive refutation and conclusion (siddhānta). The uttarapakṣa is sometimes replaced by the saṁgati which consists of establishing relations with the context. (L. Renou, *op. cit.*, II, p. 15.)

With regard to the "non-human" origin of the Veda and its traditional authority, the Mīmāṁsā has developed the theory of the eternity of sound. "Śabda, which is both sound and word, is, like ether (ākāśa), indefinitely present as a latent power. This is one of the essential postulates of the system. Eternal sound is to empirical sound as being to manifestation." (Renou, *idem.*)

For an understanding of texts the Mīmāṁsā stresses the necessity of correct spelling and correct pronunciation, as well as the obligation of clearly distinguishing the different classes of mantra according to their appropriate rhythms.

This darśana, the Mīmāṁsā, is a rigorous discipline and full of valuable information. It is an exegesis of the Brāhmaṇas as the Vedānta is of the Upaniṣads.

THE SIXTH DARŚANA: THE VEDĀNTA

The Vedānta means the end, the conclusion of the Vedas. It is the last of the six orthodox darśanas and completes the Upaniṣads with which the Vedic texts end. The Upaniṣads represent the foundations which the Vedānta completes and crowns with its own structure, for the primordial tradition expressed in the Upaniṣads, the criterion *par excellence* of truth, since it is Śruti, constitutes the very essence of Vedāntic doctrine. The Vedānta is the exegesis of the Upaniṣads as the Mīmāṁsā is the exegesis of the Brāhmaṇas. It is, moreover, called the second Mīmāṁsā.

The principal teachings of the Vedānta, attributed to the ṛṣi Bādarāyaṇa or Vyāsa, author of the Epics and of the Purāṇas, have been grouped into a synthesis or collection of very concise aphorisms known as the Brahmasūtras and the Śārīraka-mīmāṁsā.

The five great commentators of the Vedāntic school are Śaṁkara, Rāmānuja, Nimbārka, Madhva and Vallabha. But the most famous of the commentaries to which the Brahmasūtras have given birth is that of Saṁkara, often called Saṁkarācārya. "His important commentary", writes Louis Renou, "is one of the great products of Indian philosophy."

This is a real doctrine of pure metaphysics and opens limitless vistas to spiritual speculation. It is not a closed system—on the contrary. Its perspectives stretch into the universal and the infinite. The basis of the doctrine depends upon the concept of the unity of spiritual reality and upon the relations between the supreme Self or Brahman and the individual self or ātman.

The path of knowledge taught in the Upaniṣads can be summarized as follows:

> the ātman is Brahman.
> so 'ham: I am he.
> tat tvam asi: thou art that.

Inherent in this formula are all the subsequent developments of philosophy and metaphysics, the seed of truths that will fertilize spiritual life throughout the centuries.

The great mantra "tat tvam asi" or "thou art that" was expounded by Śaṁkara about A.D. 800. It constitutes the credo of the Advaita or "non-dualism" of Śaṁkara. Only the One exists. The manifested world is an illusion, an empirical reality only. If we live in God, the manifestation disappears; if we live in the world, God no longer exists. In this connection the classical example of the serpent must not be omitted. A length of rope on a roadway at night looks like a serpent. The rope itself is not seen. At daybreak the rope is seen and the serpent has disappeared.

The system of Śaṁkara proves the identity of the jīva, the individual soul, with Brahman, the universal soul. This does not mean that the jīva is equal to God (Brahman). The identity is not established in empirical terms, for the part cannot be held to equal the whole. But the substrate which exists in the jīva and in the universe is everywhere the same. Thus we observe the ontological aspect and perceive the "real essence of the real."

"Manifestation (nature or māyā) has but an inferior station; it is the substrate alone (which is necessary for an illusion to arise) that is absolutely real. Hence in empirical reality there is an indefinable mixture of existence and non-existence." (Swami Siddhesvarananda, *Quelques aspects de la philosophie védantique.*)

According to the central thesis of Vedānta (the relation of Brahman and ātman) it can be said that three different aspects exist both in the individual (microcosm) and in the phenomenal world (macrocosm):

Gross aspect: vaiśvānara (individual), Virāṭ (universal).
Subtle aspect: taijasa (individual), Hiraṇyagarbha (universal).
Causal aspect: prajña (individual), Īśvara (universal).

Virāṭ represents the totality of animate beings.

Hiraṇyagarbha is the totality of individual spirits or cosmic mind-force, i.e., universal life.

Īśvara is the God who contains in himself the entire phenomenal world. And beyond these three degrees, beyond the non-manifest in the causal state, where are gathered all the possibilities of life, he exists—the unconditioned, the incomprehensible, the unthinkable, the inexpressible Brahman.

Brahman is the support of the universe as the ātman is of the individual.

To understand the Vedānta properly it is necessary first of all to postulate the distinction of the Self, the principle of Being, with that of the individual. The Self, a transcendent, permanent and immutable principle is never affected by the transient individuality it adopts. It never becomes individualized. It can certainly undergo unlimited developments through an indefinite gamut of possibilities as a result of its empirical manifestation but its permanence is never affected. The Self is the principle whereby all states of being can exist in their appropriate fields.

Vedānta leads to release "by which the unity of the individual is finally and consciously attained. It reabsorbs the jīva and Brahman into itself and banishes avidyā 'ignorance' and karma" (Renou).

After Śaṁkara the most eminent commentator of the Brahmasūtras was Rāmānuja. His commentary, the Śrībhāṣya, is a considerable work. His approach is different from that of Śaṁkara. His leading idea is that unity does not reside in a single principle but in distinct parts surrounding that principle. In their turn, Madhva and Nimbārka have expounded other theses on a dualist basis, whereas Vallabha created the śuddhādvaita or "pure non-dualism".

In its various schools the Vedānta has always tried to conserve or gain better understanding of the ancient wisdom of Vedic revelation by means of commentaries which are strictly orthodox within the framework of the six darśanas.

Śaṁkara, the great spokesman of the Vedānta declares: "Since all proceeds from the Self and all resolves itself into the Self and since, during the intermediate stage of conservation, everything remains imbued with the Self, for this reason the Self cannot be apprehended unless it be by itself and consequently all is the Self." (From the commentaries of Śaṁkarācārya, quoted by Swami Siddhesvarananda, *Essais sur la métaphysique du Védanta*, p. 66.)

The path of liberation that is Vedānta leads to the realization of the Absolute, which is here described in the words of Śaṁkara's Vivekacūḍāmaṇi, where it treats of the man liberated in life, the jīvanmukta.

"He whose mind is merged in Brahman; who retains his alertness, though free from the characteristics of the waking state; whose understanding is without desires, he is thought of as a jīvanmukta.

"He who has stilled all care brought by the phenomenal world and is undivided in himself, though his (physical) parts (pursue their different functions); he who is free from fear, such a man is a jīvanmukta.

"He ignores the thought of 'I and mine', even though his body follows him like a shadow. Such a man is a jīvanmukta."

(Vivekacūḍāmaṇi, 429–31.)

CHAPTER VI

THE DIVINE

It fell to the lot of pure poetry, singing of the cosmic forces of heaven and earth, to give to the world the conception of the Absolute as revealed in the Veda, from earliest times the book of traditional knowledge in India. This Absolute is Brahman which cannot be defined. Brahman, the brilliant light of lights "contained in its golden sheath", by means of which the mind thinks, but which itself cannot be seized by thought, remains beyond all communication. "You ask what Brahman is? It is your own ātman which is within all things" (Bṛhad Āraṇyaka Up. III. 4).

Brahman, neutral and impersonal, is unconditioned, unqualified and indistinguishable. It is the origin, the cause, the essence of the universe, for all that it is Brahman. It is pure being (sat), pure intelligence (cit) and pure bliss (ānanda). Since Brahman cannot be grasped in its entirety and truth, the Hindus try to seek it in its divine manifestations. To worship Brahman in its attributes is to bring it down to a human level and place it within reach. Thus Brahman assumes the form of a personal god. It can be contemplated in any of its functions or powers.

In the Vedic hymns the gods addressed are scarcely endowed with human features but belong rather to the stars, the atmosphere and the earth. Their names and aspects are innumerable, for they are all expressions of Brahman, limitless in its forms but One in its essence. These divine manifestations echo the affinities of the faithful. Their multiplicity astonishes the western mind all the more because each personified god is sometimes known by several names which vary according to the quality or activity for which he is invoked. The god selected by his worshipper is known as his iṣṭa and it is to him that the worshipper offers his prayers and rosaries and through him that he approaches Brahman, the Supreme Divinity, of which all the gods are but intermediaries. Brahman comprehends all iṣṭas. They are always Brahman, since *all* is Brahman.

The gods may personify forces of nature as well as Joy, Mercy or Death. To show him that all these manifestations are but the one Brahman seen through the eyes of the fervent devotee, Viṣṇu says to Śiva in the Viṣṇu Purāṇa: "Those whom ignorance holds in thrall consider me as separate from thee."

The believer may find Brahman within himself in his heart, for every being possesses a spark of Brahman. This is known as ātman and this ātman is the Self of each man, a transcendental principle which never becomes individualized. "Brahman dwells within the heart. It is there and not elsewhere. Wise men who study it within their hearts, but no others, acquire eternal rest" (Bṛhad Āraṇyaka Upaniṣad).

In the highly complex and elaborately evolved mythology of the Veda, the most frequently invoked gods include, foremost, Indra who embodies conquering strength. His feats and victories are the subject-matter of numerous stories. With his thunderbolt (vajra) he slew the dragon which obstructed the waters and, after conquering the sun, he released the captive dawns.

The steed (vahana) of Indra is a white elephant called Airāvata. Generally the god is depicted as bedecked with jewels, wearing the royal turban or the cylindrical tiara and holding the thunderbolt, the disk and the elephant tusk. His wife is Indrāṇī or Śacī whom he kidnapped from her father, his enemy Puloman.

Rudra, the "powerful one" of the Vedic hymns, later became Śiva, the beneficent and healing god. The Rudras, sons of Rudra, together with Indra form a group of youths who ride the clouds, bringing in their wake storms and rain.

Agni, the god of fire and sacrifice, has a very important function. He unites the three parts of the universe: earth, heaven and the atmosphere between. He is at the same time the divine will, the perfect vision and the ritual performance:

> O Agni, thou art the substance of young shoots and the waters are thy seed. Innate in all things, growing together with them, thou leadest them to ripeness. The whole exists in thee. Thou clothest thyself as the sun and with thy rays thou drawest water from the earth; then, by the rains which thou pourest forth in their season, thou restorest life to all beings. The all is reborn through thee: the creeper, the green leaves, lakes and the fertile bed of the waters, the whole of that watery palace over which Varuṇa holds sway (Rigveda).

Varuṇa, the preserver of cosmic order and the lord of the waters, is one of the principal gods of the Vedic religion. With this god, who is draped in a golden mantle, is associated Mitra in an aura of juridical majesty and with a retinue of seven or eight entities called the Ādityas, who are descendants of the mother-goddess Aditi. Sūrya, the sun, becomes Vivasvant, while the moon is Candra and the wind Vāyu. Prajāpati, the father of the gods (devas) and the demons (asuras), lord of all creatures, is an important figure in the hierarchy of the gods and many hymns are addressed to him.

Of secondary importance are Dyauṣpitṛ, "heaven father", and Pṛthivī, the Earth Mother, the Maruts, tempest divinities, Uṣas, the Dawn and the Aśvins who symbolize the morning and evening stars. Yama, the first man, became the god of death and the master of the underworld. Then comes Pūṣan, the god who guides both men and beasts. Of him our picture is less clear. Bṛhaspati, the priest of the gods, is another aspect of Agni. It is impossible to list all the Vedic gods, for they are countless. Apart from the gods, the most powerful force in the universe is ṛta which is at the same time the cosmic, ritual and moral order.

Finally there is soma, the sacrificial plant. This becomes a fermented liquor which has assumed the importance of a divine drink conferring immortality upon the drinker and in Book IX of the Rigveda it has even been elevated to the status of a god.

"The origin of Soma upon earth is on a mountain, upon Mt. Mūjavant. But its true home is the sky; it is a child of heaven whose celestial form is suited to its birth and the manner of its pressing. It was brought down to this earth by a great bird, an eagle or a falcon, which snatched it from the brazen castle in which it was being guarded by the Gandharvas or the archer Kṛśānu who fired at the bird, ripping from it a claw or a feather. Sometimes the eagle is Indra; in the Brāhmaṇas it is Gāyatri (Agni under his mystical name) who steals the soma" (L. Renou, *op. cit.*, p. 329).

A divine trinity or Trimūrti stands at the head of the manifold divine forms. Three gods make up this trinity and share the basic activities of Īśvara, the generic name of the one supreme god or the Will of Power symbolizing the neutral and unknowable Brahman who stands above the trinity.

The power to create, which appears to be the most lofty function, is proper to Brahmā who is not to be confused with the impersonal Brahman. Brahmā, on the contrary, becomes a personal god by reason of his creative function.

Then comes the power of preservation which is in the hands of Viṣṇu. And, finally, Śiva wields the power to destroy. These gods, who represent the three aspects of Īśvara, make up the Trimūrti or great trinity of India, whose activity corresponds to the rhythm of the creation of the world: the beginning of a cycle, its full manifestation and its ending and reabsorption into Brahman or the pralaya, the period preceding the next age.

The relations of the gods amongst themselves are as vague and unstable as a legend with its variants. Nevertheless, certain well-established myths remain constant and are always connected with a particular god or goddess. The god does not change but man's heart grows and thus makes to grow within him his conception of the god.

Amongst the important gods who replaced or supplemented the Vedic gods in Indian tradition, Brahmā remains fairly abstract notwithstanding his function as creator. It is he who brings into being "diversity within unity". No particular cult is devoted to him and his sanctuaries are few. The greatest of them is at Pushkar, near Ajmer in Rajputana. Sarasvatī is the śakti of Brahmā. Śakti is the energy that emanates from the god to complement him with a female divine form. Sarasvatī, who is found associated with the great gods and is identified in the Brāhmaṇas with the Word (vāc), was, at the Vedic period, the goddess of the sacred rivers and is the symbol of the arts, eloquence, knowledge and the "waters of Truth".

Brahmā is often depicted with four faces (caturmukha) turned towards the points of the compass and with four arms with the hands holding the four Vedas. His heads are crowned or have plaited hair (whence his name of śikhin) and the faces are bearded. His attributes are the ewer, the rosary, the two ritual spoons (mānasāra) and sometimes the disk. His colour is pink. Sometimes he rides on a swan (haṁsa), sometimes he stands and more often he sits upon a lotus which is emerging from Viṣṇu's belly—hence his name "born of a lotus" or "he of the navel". Since the epic period he has also borne the name "he that has issued from himself" (svayaṁbhū) that is to say, he that is innate (L. Renou, *op. cit.*, p. 500).

Viṣṇu in the Trimūrti performs the beneficent rôle of preserver of the cosmos. He presides over human fate. He is a god of solar origin and is characterized by the four attributes: the shell (śaṅkha), the disk (cakra), the club (gadā) and the lotus flower (padma). Viṣṇu is depicted as a youth, deep blue in colour and with four arms.

"The twenty-four niṣṭhās or 'attitudes' which make up the picture of the god in its totality have each an esoteric value which determines a particular incarnation. Also informed with symbolic meaning are the jewel kaustubha, which Viṣṇu wears round his neck, the curled hair stylized in art and the śrīvatsa which adorns his breast. His head is generally surmounted by a diadem (kirīṭa)" (L. Renou, *ibid.*).

Viṣṇu is depicted reclining or even sleeping upon a chaotic ocean, the infinite thousand-headed serpent. Or he can be seen presiding in heaven as Vaikuṇṭha surrounded by his court. Viṣṇu's steed (vahana) is Garuḍa, himself an object of worship. This Garuḍa is the heavenly eagle, the son of Kaśyapa and Vinatā. It is Garuḍa who snatched from the gods' use the drink of life or soma.

The very popular cult of Viṣṇu boasts a multiplicity of forms and numerous sanctuaries. Viṣṇu is also venerated on a very lofty abstract plane, for he is the symbol of divine love. Viṣṇu is often escorted by his śakti who is Lakṣmī or "Beauty and Fortune", the emblem of the ideal and ministering wife as well as being the symbol of honour and prosperity. She is depicted as a captivating young woman, seated upon a lotus and holding an horn of plenty, while two white elephants bearing ewers in their trunks water the lotuses in her hands. She is invoked for spiritual and temporal benefits, faith and health.

In the Hindu tradition the gods may be reincarnated either of their own free will or by order to fulfil a mission, especially that of bringing aid to humanity in distress. The divine incarnations are known as avatars (avatāra) or "descents". Viṣṇu is the god who most frequently becomes incarnate. The number of possible avatars is unlimited. Ramakrishna said: "Avatars are to Brahman as waves are to the ocean."

When an important god comes down to earth, lesser divinities accompany him and make up his retinue. Numerous incarnations of Viṣṇu are described in the Bhāgavata Purāṇa but only ten are classical. The first shows Viṣṇu coming in the form of a fish to save king Manu Vaivasvata. This is the Indian story of the great Flood. Then Viṣṇu appears as a wild boar. He lifts up the Earth which the demon Hiraṇyākṣa had submerged in the depths of the ocean. It is once more Viṣṇu, in the guise of Rāma, the hero of the Rāmāyaṇa, who triumphs over the demon Rāvaṇa. Finally, serving as a pedestal at the bottom of the seas, Viṣṇu, in the shape of a tortoise, holds up Mount Meru which is encircled by the serpent Śeṣa. He is present at the churning of the ocean. In this combat between the gods and the Asuras, marvellous treasures are at stake, in particular the amṛta or divine drink. Thanks to Viṣṇu the gods carry the day.

The most famous of Viṣṇu's avatars—and all his avatars have an esoteric meaning—is that of Kṛṣṇa who is considered as a total incarnation whereas usually incarnations are only partial. The life of Kṛṣṇa is a series of extraordinary adventures. Kṛṣṇa, chief of the Yādava clan, possessing incredible powers (he had already accomplished prodigious feats as a child), pursues his career as a superhuman being. As an adolescent he is the divine cowherd who plays the flute among shepherdesses who dance around him and contemplate him with amorous fervour. This scene occurs in the sacred wood of Vṛndāvana.

Later, in the Bhagavadgītā, he fights at the side of his cousins, the Pāṇḍavas, in their war against the Bhāratas. There he distinguishes himself by showing, by example and precept, how man must develop spiritually in order to attain liberation. As Rāma, symbolizing mental energy and as Kṛṣṇa, standing for divine inspiration, Viṣṇu brings considerable aid to humanity and plays an important part in Indian religion. Viṣṇu is a saviour, for, "in each of his avatars he recovers things which seemed irrevocably lost, swallowed up or about to be swallowed up by the ocean, that is, by the undifferentiated" (Herbert, *spiritualité hindoue*, p. 262).

Whether in the form of Rāma's wife Sītā, in the Rāmāyaṇa, or of Kṛṣṇa's favourite shepherdess Rādhā, who is one of the most popular figures of all the feminine divinities as well as Kṛṣṇa's most devoted adorer, it is always Lakṣmī, Viṣṇu's śakti and the goddess of harmony, who is found incarnate together with him.

Śiva is a complex and ambivalent god, at the same time beneficent and to be feared. Here the double aspect of divine activity is to be observed. In the Hindu trinity, Śiva is the destroyer but he annihilates only in order to rebuild. He destroys that multiplicity which is the created world in order to recreate unity. For this reason he is confused with Time (kāla) for, like him, he builds and destroys in an unending succession. Is it not he who deposited in the depths of the sea the "Golden Seed which encloses Brahman", while remaining at the same time "he that carries away" and that in his most fearful form of Bhairava or "Terror" in all its sixty-four kinds?

But, on the other hand, he possesses the quality of restorer and he is also a protector invoked in time of danger. In the episode of the churning of the sea of milk (the emergence of the world in all its forms), when the serpent Vāsuki emitted a venom intended to destroy the earth, Śiva drank the poison. His throat became blue-black and hence he was named Nīlakaṇṭha. It was also Śiva who, when the waters of the Ganges flowed down upon the earth, offered himself up in order to avert a catastrophe. He bound his hair in a high protective knot (jaṭa) and received the rushing waters which then flowed away harmlessly.

Śiva is a god endowed with immeasurable power (the Rudra of the hymns) for he is the god of life and procreation. But Śiva is above all the Mahādeva, the great ascetic god, guide and model for the Yogins whom he brings to consciousness of Unity. He is known as Mahāyogin, "master of the Yogins". "He is portrayed half-naked, smeared with ashes, girt with skulls and wearing a necklace of snakes (already in the Vedic religion Rudra was the lord of snakes . . .). His posture is one of meditation and he has a third eye in his forehead caused, it would appear, when Pārvatī one day had playfully covered his eyes with her hand" (L. Renou, *op. cit.*, p. 514).

He is most often to be found as the Nāṭarāja, many-armed, dancing the Tāṇḍava or cosmic dance, surrounded with the tiruvāśi or halo of fire. It is said that he is trampling upon a rebel demon or that he is destroying the world in order to recreate it. Indeed this dance readily brings to mind many symbols of esoteric meaning.

The customary mount of Śiva is the white bull Nandin and his garment is the tiger-skin. He wears as a diadem the crescent moon and his attributes are the bow (ajagava), the drum (ḍhakkā), the club Khaṭvāṅga, the snare (pāśa) and, most commonly, the trident (triśūla Pināka). Śiva has four, eight or sixteen arms, the bottom pair of which makes the gesture of favour (varada) and of protection (abhaya). Innumerable sanctuaries have been identified as belonging to Śiva. Those of Bhuvaneshvar and Madura are world-famous.

Śiva delegates his power to numerous śaktis: Pārvatī, daughter of the mountain, Satī, the faithful wife, Umā the beneficent, Caṇḍī, the violent one, and others. The most important of them all, Durgā or Kālī, the terrible goddess, is depicted under a fearsome aspect. She is dark and naked, with windblown hair and she wears a necklace of human heads and tramples under foot the body of her husband, while she waves aloft a bloody knife and a head recently cut off. This Kālī is, nonetheless, an aspect of the divine Mother, the Supreme One. She embodies robust energy and implacable will-power and, like her husband, Śiva, seems to destroy only in order to release the spirituality within each being. When ignorance is abolished, the heart becomes pure. The strength of Kālī creates peace after it has destroyed ignorance. The strength of Kālī is terrible in action but when it reaches the "heart" of Śiva, that is, when illusion is banished, Kālī suddenly stops and in the flash of comprehension bites her tongue. She starts to bleed and asks herself: "What has this wild impulse made me do?" She has attained reality and now becomes balanced, calm and gentle.

In Durgā are united Kālī, Lakṣmī and Sarasvatī, the three guṇas which represent destruction, evolution and creation. The "severed heads" symbolize the demons of ignorance in humanity. Kālī adopts souls thus released as a personal adornment. She has freed them from ignorance and fear. Durgā-Kālī was Ramakrishna's chosen divinity.

The Indians give to paintings and statues of their gods a human face and adorn them with distinguishing emblems. Superhuman power is indicated by extra arms—two, four or even more. The symbol of divine sight is a third eye placed, as in Śiva's case, in the middle of the forehead; Brahmā has four heads. Animal characteristics are indicative of special qualities. Thus it is with Gaṇeśa who has an elephant's head and the Kiṁnaras who have horses' heads.

Gaṇeśa, the chief of the Gaṇas (divine troops), is the object of a fervent cult. He is the son of Śiva and Pārvatī. His aid is sought before every enterprise, for he is the guide (vināyaka) who levels all obstacles. Gaṇeśa symbolizes the appeal to spiritual strength. The part he plays in the Rāmāyaṇa is a good example of his spirit of sacrifice, perseverance and dedication.

Gaṇeśa is depicted with an elephant's head and a single tusk. His colour is generally red but he can also be white or yellow. He has a protruding belly and his mount is a rat or a lion. He carries an elephant tusk and a rosary. His popularity is widespread, especially in the south, and images of him can be seen at crossroads, beneath trees and in temples.

The monkey Hanumān, the symbol of dexterity and intelligence, is the son of the wind god Pavana. He is considered, amongst all the divinities of India, to be the "perfect servant" of Brahman since he exemplifies strength and self-control. He is allied with Rāma, the leader of the monkey army, and numerous temples are dedicated to him.

GENII AND DEMONS

A world of supernatural beings, genii and demons, form the retinue of this array of major and minor gods and lesser divinities of the Hindu religion who are all so many aspects of the single divinity. They can change their shape at will and are usually grouped under a leader. Their influence can be good or harmful—sometimes both at once.

Asuras, Daityas and other similar demons are among the most harmful of these beings who stand half-way between gods and men. The heroes of the epics do battle with them. The Nāgas or "serpents" belong to the shades of the earth. They are underground genii depicted with a human head and a serpent's tail. The Yakṣas and the Yakṣiṇīs are "guardians of wealth and magical illusions".

The Gandharvas, musicians and dancers, who are not unlike Fauns, are found in association with the Apsarasas or water-nymphs who dance and play and are sometimes connected with tree cults. The best known is Urvaśī who is the heroine of a legend in which king Purūravas figures. Rāvaṇa, the demon prince, is at the same time the patron of an anti-demonic ritual. In reality, devils do not play a great part in the Veda and evil only occasionally appears to exist. It is a mere shadow, the negative aspect of the ambivalence of a spirit or an ordinary man. The Indians attribute to certain animals a sacred character. The cow is the sacred animal *par excellence*.

One cult, whose forms have become restricted though they may still vary, worships the snake. The snake, which is much revered, has suggested many symbols. When it bites its own tail, it evokes eternity; when it issues from the mouth of a sleeper, it suggests the escaping soul. The swan (haṁsa) is the customary steed of Brahmā and represents the soul as identified with the sun.

The elephant symbolizes wisdom and strength and is one of the most important sacred animals. Its origin is held to be miraculous and its species provides the four and, subsequently, the eight Guardians of the World or Lokapālas. The four rulers of the world who stood beneath Mount Meru were seated upon four cosmic elephants, the Diṅnāgas.

For the Indians the difference between men and animals is merely one of evolutionary progress. They therefore treat animals with a touching solicitude in order to help on their development. But the cow is particularly sacred in India. It was already important in the Veda as the symbol of light. "The Vedic cow, a basically enigmatic animal, comes from no earthly herd. The word 'go' means both 'cow' and 'light'. Cows are the rays of the dawn, the herds of the sun; they are no cattle of flesh and blood. The lost cows are the lost rays of the sun; their recovery heralds the recovery of the lost sun" (Śrī Aurobindo, *op. cit.*).

The feeling for what is sacred, which the Indian people possess in the highest degree, may extend to trees, plants and stones for, in their eyes, nature also takes on religious forms. But water is especially sacred by reason of its purificatory function. The holiest river is the Ganges, which "crosses heaven in the form of a celestial river or the milky way", then reaches earth and finally hell. Every Hindu prays that he might die at Benares, on the banks of the Ganges.

CHAPTER VII

CREATION

Hindu metaphysics depends entirely upon the concept of a single substance animated by a single rhythm with pre-established harmonies. This concept explains the theory of the macrocosm and the microcosm or the theory that links the human organism to the exterior world or cosmos by a series of points of resemblance. The body corresponds to the earth, speech to fire, air to breath, the eye to the sun and so forth. Collectively the gods are the celestial body of which Indra is the head, Rudra the hand, Agni the mouth, Varuṇa the belly, Sūrya the right eye, Candra the left, Vāyu the limbs, Prajāpati the reproductive organs, the Maruts the respiration of the gods, and finally Dyaus the cavities of the heart. Though microscopically so, the human body is made after the image of the great divine body.

The rhythm of life and death is like the great cosmic rhythm of the universal manifestation of Brahman and like the pralaya or universal dissolution and cosmic slumber. Creation is only a passing from the unmanifest to the manifest, from the many to the one.

It is by a single inspiration of breath that Brahman creates the universe and by a single expiration that he annihilates and reabsorbs it into himself. Brahman breathes eternally, creating and destroying, without interrupting the existence of the universe, the cosmos and boundless space.

The creative process starts in the form of "non-knowledge" or "ignorance", the eternal and unmanifested substrate. From this first state arises ahaṁkāra or "essence of individualization". From this essence emerges the spirit or consciousness of the individual self (asmitā) and then comes an imponderable material continuum known as the "fore-established" (pradhāna) which extends over all space and carries within itself the three guṇas. These three guṇas qualify the primordial substance. They are: sattva, the principle of light, rajas, the affective and impure principle, tamas, the principle of darkness.

The material continuum called ākāśa "ether", which is of extreme subtlety, gives birth to the four elements: air, fire, water and earth. From a combination of these proceeds life, which is the egg of Brahman. From this egg, deposited in the depths of the waters, comes forth all creation. The phenomenal world is given shape physically and psychologically by a mixture of the three guṇas and the four elements together with ākāśa. This mixture gives form to material bodies of increasing density. Sattva directs the soul towards Brahman while rajas and tamas turn it away. It is the guṇas that govern the unequal nature of human activity, the world of names and forms or the conscious, immanent and transcendental dream of Brahman. Just as all things are Brahman, reside in him and are part of him, so, in the same way, drops of water are part of the ocean. The world is Brahman but Brahman serves as ātman to the universe.

Brahman is unmanifest in the early stage when the as yet potential world of names and forms has not emerged from sleep. He is the cause. In the second stage Brahman is manifest and is the effect and this interplay of causes and effects, of puruṣa and prakṛti, is none other than cosmic motion itself. The manifest Brahman alternates for all eternity with the unmanifest Brahman. The universal dissolution or pralaya enables it to be said that all effects are unreal since they are reabsorbed into their causes.

"This same sum of born beings, rising to birth after birth, dissolves away without will of its own at the coming of Night . . ." (Bhagavadgītā, VIII, 19).[1]

The infinite substance ākāśa, which is life, shapes the universe. It evolves through man as far as the gods. Hence a stone may live, suffer and die. The force that impels ākāśa is prāṇa or "energy". To the Hindu mind, matter is simply energy in a state of motion

[1] L. D. Barnett trans., *Bhagavadgītā*, London, 1905.

or energy which is differentiated. This is the theory of evolution itself. All evolves, even man who is the focal point of all becoming. For man, who is endowed with freedom, can break out from the cycle of rebirth (saṁsāra) when he has grasped the illusory nature of matter. He then discovers himself to be part of Brahman and he exerts himself to break the round of existence in order to return to Brahman.

This illusory nature of matter is called māyā. But this almost untranslatable term is generally misinterpreted. It does not exactly mean "illusion" but is rather to be seen as the antithesis of the noumen. It is the veil concealing Absolute Reality, the stage-set for the comedy in which men are the actors, the play of Lord Kṛṣṇa, the hidden spring that sets going the transformation of humanity for the greater glory of the divine.

The Hindus regard the appearance and disappearance of the world not as a unique phenomenon but as events in a rhythmic cycle. Each period between two successive creations is known as a kalpa or "day of Brahman" which, in western terms, would last about 4,320 million years. Every kalpa consists of 1,000 periods called "great ages", the perfect age or caturyuga. Each of these is made up of four "ages" or yugas which are called satya, tretā, dvāpara and kali. The last is the current yuga which has already lasted for approximately 16,000 years.

The kali yuga or "evil age" is characterized by a wastage of three-quarters of the dharma existing in the perfect age and this results in wars, plagues, vice and untimely deaths. The curve of humanity at the present time, as also that of humanity in the past and in the future, follows a regressive path, finishing in "intermediate dissolutions"—fires followed by floods. At the end of time will come the "great dissolution" (mahāpralaya) coinciding with the end of Brahmā's life span; the world will be reabsorbed into Brahman by a process of involution until such time as a new cosmic egg should begin to hatch.

"When", says the Bhāgavata, "the world is destroyed at the end of two Brahmic ages, when the gross elements are reabsorbed into the prime element, when the evolved, under the pressure of time, returns into the unevolved then, you (Viṣṇu) alone remain under the name of Śeṣa."[2]

It must be added that each kalpa is divided into fourteen "periods of Manu" or manvantaras of equal duration and over each there is a presiding Manu. In the present kalpa mankind is directed by the seventh or Manu Vaivasvata, son of the solar deity Vivasvant. In each manvantara a new series of those entitled to hold the positions of the principal gods and ṛṣis enter upon their functions.

Śrī Aurobindo describes the four ages as follows:

> [The first age] "the Satyayuga is a period of the world in which a harmony, stable and sufficient, is created and man realizes for a time, under certain conditions and limitations, the perfection of his being; [in the following age this harmony is no longer the consequence of a] settled purity; but [. . .] it begins to break down and man upholds it [. . .] by force of will, individual and collective; [in the next age man sees that] it breaks down further and he attempts to uphold it . . . by intellectual regulation and common consent. Finally, in the Age of Iron or Ignorance, through which mankind is at present passing, this harmony collapses but in it the necessary conditions are progressively built up for a new Satya, another harmony, a more advanced perfection. At the close of the kalpa there takes place the great dissolution (pratisaṁcara, mahāpralaya) in which all creation, even Śiva and Viṣṇu, disappear.[3]

[2] L. Renou, *Hindouisme*, p. 54.
[3] (Śrī Aurobindo, *The Yoga and its Objects*, pp. 3, 4, 5th edn, Calcutta, 1949. Quoted in Herbert, *Spiritualité hindoue*, p. 62.)

CHAPTER VIII

KARMA

The idea of karma, which is the central doctrine of the Sanātana Dharma, follows from the principle of causality that governs human destiny. Every act and thought produce their effect, either good or bad, for which the perpetrator, either in this life or in another, will one day have to face the consequences. Punishment may not come immediately but it is inescapable. The sum of these effects produces the karma of each being throughout the succession of his existences. It is impossible to escape this law of karma or retribution for actions.

By explaining the causes of our destiny karma justifies its consequences. We become indeed what we think or do. The present life of any individual as conditioned by his preceding one determines the next. Consciousness is a karmic memory contained by the higher conscious mind or vijñāna, for every conscious individual is, in part or in a certain way, a "descent of the Infinite" into the apparent finiteness of form and name. "The conscious, incarnate soul (dehī) is a spark of divine fire."

Under this law the heinousness of suicide becomes readily apparent. Each man must undergo his karma and not reject it by interrupting the course of his life. Suicide is a refusal to live when in fact the entire consequences of previous actions must be accepted. The expiation subsequent upon this refusal is all the heavier for having been deferred.

Karma must be lived out by extinguishing in the self all thirst for existence lest there arise new karma that would necessitate a rebirth, so that it might be fulfilled in its turn. Thus is it possible to break free from the "wheel" of births and deaths, for karma accumulates only during life.

In the law of karma is admitted the idea of a collective karma. This can affect a people, a family or any kind of human group whenever an action, collectively committed—for better or worse—in a previous existence of that group, weighs upon its destiny.

REINCARNATION

The law of karma automatically postulates the law of reincarnation as a necessity, since the soul must return to work off the "wages" of its karma. According to Vedic ideas, the soul is born and dies many times. It wraps itself in "sheaths" (koṣas) or temporary dwellings. The Bhagavadgītā states:

"As a man lays aside outworn garments and takes others that are new, so the Body-Dweller puts away outworn bodies and goes to others that are new."[1]

The life of an individual is only one in an unending sequence of lives, each one giving rise to the next and laying down the conditions by which the preceding karma or prārabdhakarma might be annulled. The chain of succeeding existences is known as saṁsāra. Since the soul cannot perish as does the body it confirms the law of karma by being reborn. "Every act bears fruit and none can be annulled."

To the objection that might be made if it is allowed that one life determines the next Śaṁkara makes this reply:

"Since saṁsāra is without beginning, works stand to the uneven nature of created things as cause to effect, as the seed to the plant."

Śaṁkara adds that all things rest in Brahman:

> In the case of the individual soul which, through ignorance, is unable to distinguish itself from the aggregate of its acts and its organs and is blinded by the shadows of ignorance, saṁsāra, both as an active and a passive principle, arises by permission of the supreme being, he that surveys all actions, the witness within all beings and the source of all spirituality. Consequently, we must admit that it is by his grace that we obtain knowledge and by means of knowledge mokṣa or "release". The scriptures express it thus: Brahman is the agent of the cause or the primal cause in all action.

[1] L. D. Barnett trans., *Bhagavadgītā*, II, 22.

At their birth men lose the recollection of their former lives. Yet for some the veil is occasionally lifted. Patañjali says:

"In truth the past and future have equal existence with the present but they cannot be seen for they are on different planes. If they did not exist, the Yogin would not see them as a result of his concentration. In the Gītā it says: 'Many are my former lives and yours also, O Arjuna. I know them all but you do not, O scourge of your enemies.' "

Various incarnations succeed one another at greater or shorter intervals as the case might be. During these intervals the soul dwells in a paradise or a hell. In these temporary abodes it harvests retribution for those good and evil actions which have not yet borne fruit. According to Swami Vivekananda it is not always necessary to die before passing from one incarnation to the next.

In his Rājayoga he says:

"The Yogins claim that men who have succeeded in acquiring a considerable store of good mental impressions (saṁskāras) do not need to die but can, in the course of this life, exchange their body for a divine body. . . . These men simply change the substance of their bodies by a redistribution of the molecules."

But these are exceptional beings who have reached not only the pinnacle of spiritual development but also the enlightenment that crowns it.

In order to put an end to karma it is necessary to prevent the accumulation of more. Now with every thought more is added to what has already piled up. Kṛṣṇa, a divine incarnation, shows a way out of that terrifying prospect. He declares:

27. "Whatever be thy work, thine eating, thy sacrifice, thy gift, thy mortification, make thou of it an offering to me, O son of Kuntī.

28. "Thus shalt thou be released from the bonds of Works, fair or foul of fruit; thy spirit inspired by casting-off of Works and following the Rule, thou shalt be delivered and come to me."[2]

By offering to the godhead every action, thought and word,

[2] *Bhagavadgītā*, IX, 27, 28. Trans. L. D. Barnett.

karma is brought to an end. Any thought of merit in this dedication is a trap. Total self-forgetfulness is necessary before the divine power can act; all personal tastes and dislikes must be cast aside. Individual desires and aspirations must disappear for ever in the face of the supreme Will. The task here required is known as dharma.

DHARMA

Dharma, the fundamental idea of Hinduism and closely linked with karma, is equally important with it. The very name of the Hindu religion—Sanātana Dharma—means eternal or universal dharma. Dharma may be considered as the "mainstay" of beings and things, the law of order in its widest sense, that is, of cosmic order. But it is at the same time a law of moral order and of religious merit—in fact, the pure notion of personal duty.

In order to obtain the experience which it lacks, the human soul, when called upon to live a new existence on earth, is placed in the most favourable conditions. If it fulfils the rôle assigned it by its karma, it obeys the laws of universal harmony. If it resists and simply follows the dictates of its own egoism, it wastes its efforts and has to suffer the consequences.

By fulfilling dharma the soul works off its residue of karma and escapes the endless round of rebirth and thus the law of causality. Each soul has its own individual dharma, determined by race, caste, family and private aspirations. From out of the variety of modes of behaviour every man must discover his own and follow it as an ineluctable inner law. The Brāhman has not the same dharma as the kṣatriya. The universe rests upon cosmic dharma and man upon his individual dharma. It is this latter that draws him towards a higher life.

"Whatever makes devotion to me increase is dharma", said Kṛṣṇa.

Arduous though dharma may sometimes be, no one is ever subjected to trials above his endurance. Man is invisibly sustained when bad times beset him and, more tangibly, he is assisted by the intervention of his guru or "spiritual master".

This guru is sent forth at the exact moment when the human being is in a state to accept and understand the message brought to him.

Of all the inestimable aids which the guru brings to the soul in distress, one of the most precious is the mantra. This prayer—each man possesses his own—is a powerful aid, endowed with spiritual efficacy. The guru, by his advice and his experience, guides his disciple or chela towards the state of jīvanmukti (living freedom).

When questioned about the strength of divine love, a famous guru plunged his disciple's head into the river and held it under until he almost suffocated. When the disciple emerged the guru asked him:

" 'What were you thinking about?'

" 'My whole being was bent upon breathing. I desired only that and I could think of nothing else.'

" 'Very well,' replied his master, 'when you pant equally after God you will be free.' "

RELEASE

The aim *par excellence* of the Hindu religion is to help man to release, to liberation from saṁsāra through the certainty of his identity as an individual with the Absolute, that is to say, through his knowledge that the ātman is a fragment of Brahman. "The soul, being only Brahman, merges into Brahman" (Chāndogya Up. VIII).

In order to break the fatal chain of transmigration all desire must be extinguished in the self, for desire contains the seed and the root of existence. Where desire no longer exists, the ātman, delivered from terrestrial bonds, returns to Brahman. He that obtains mokṣa (release) is one that has been freed in his own lifetime, namely a jīvanmukti. The whole of nature has become his ātman. He perceives the spirit which pervades all things both within and without. He is able to feel that his strength comes not from himself but from God. What are the paths which lead to release? Several paths are open to the believer and are described in the Sanātana Dharma.

The path of action, with a strict observance of rites, the fulfilment of pilgrimages as acts of faith, recitation of prayers at specified hours—all this represents the first step up the ladder of purification which leads to release. This path has been considered by many as inferior and inadequate. Ascetic practices and sacrifices are judged to be more efficacious. Thus the path of initiation can and ought to supplement the path of action in order to intensify its results.

The path of initiation, which involves an intensified interior devotion, provides some sects with the necessary "talisman" which devolves upon the privileged among the adepts. It consists in the "consecration" of the Tantric student, the eightfold sacrament of the Liṅgāyats and the holy dance of the Vallabhācāryas.

The way of knowledge consists in living the spiritual experience revealed by the Veda—the recognition of truth. It is the enlightenment which may suddenly invade the mind or be slowly born like an inner light which gradually kindles and, by the annihilation of the normal consciousness of the waking state, leads to ecstasy.

Side by side with these paths exist precise practical methods of spiritual training which go back to very ancient times. These methods have, of course, been progressively developed and thoroughly tried over the centuries, and are collectively known as Yoga.

CHAPTER IX

THE YOGAS

A collection of extremely ancient disciplines, known as Yoga, is one of the paths leading to release. It adopts numerous guises and techniques. Perhaps it is more of a *praxis* for salvation than a philosophy; at any rate its technical side plays a leading part in it.

Certain elements of Yoga are found in Vedic texts but an even greater antiquity than that has been attributed to the system. The various ascetic and practical theories were drawn up into a darśana, which became orthodox in the Vedāntic period, called Yoga. It is the complementary darśana to the Sāṁkhya and has special application to the Haṭha Yoga. But the Yoga is theistic whereas the Sāṁkhya is not.

Several Upaniṣads mention Yoga, for example the Taittirīya Upaniṣad and especially the Kaṭha which defines it as "the firm restraint of the senses". In addition the most characteristic exercise of Yoga, the discipline of breath, was certainly worked out as an application of theories of the physiology of breath as developed in the later Vedic literature and discussed in the Āyurveda. The purpose stated in the Yogasūtras is the same for all the Yogas, namely, to free oneself from the determinism of transmigration.

The starting-point of the system is to begin by a course of fairly severe physical training which consists in a prolonged immobility accompanied by control of breathing and of the eye muscles. These initial rules help to gain concentration—the basic condition for entering upon the way of Yoga, for concentration bears a direct relationship with knowledge. Now metaphysical fulfilment, the final aim of Yoga, consists in identification, by means of knowledge, with the Absolute.

By suppression of the passions and detachment from all that is exterior to him, the ascetic attains superior states of unshakeable stability which eventually end in mystical communion, in a state of samādhi, with the essence of his soul.

In their ślokas, which are a classification of the functions of the mind, the Yogasūtras go more deeply into the idea of samādhi and describe what it is. They distinguish two kinds of samādhi—a samādhi not yet divorced from consciousness and a second, unconscious or supra-conscious, samādhi.

The state of samādhi is the culmination of Yoga and beyond it lies release. It is a suspension of all intellectual processes that lead to instability. Samādhi, then, is a "state without apprehension". The life of the soul is not destroyed but is reduced to its "unconscious and permanent" essence. Yoga is, properly speaking, union with the self.

When thus "isolated", mind is the same as puruṣa when it is freed from mental impressions "like a precious stone isolated from its veinstone". Yoga is thus the empirical verification of the distinction postulated by the Sāṁkhya between puruṣa and prakṛti. The first is clearly distinct from the second since a psychological technique exists that is capable of separating the one from the other.

This exceptional state of samādhi is graded according to the extent of detachment from the domination of the world achieved by the Yogin. He may stop at intermediate stages—those treated in the Yogaśāstra—or pass beyond them all at once in order to achieve his final goal.

The Yogas fall into categories as according to the spiritual path one chooses at the outset but the end remains the same. The thousand years old experience of the Hindus leads them to classify Yogic adepts into several kinds. After examining the candidate, the guru, or spiritual guide, prescribes the path of Yogic development that seems best suited to his pupil's physical and mental capacities. It is an absolute rule that no lone adventures are allowed in Yogic exercises.

THE STAGES OF YOGA

The upward progress of the Yogin towards the supreme end is made up of eight stages, known in the Sūtras as Yogāṅgas. They are as follows:

(1) Yama (moral virtues); (2) Niyama (rules and observances); (3) Āsana (bodily postures); (4) Prāṇāyāma (control of the life force); (5) Pratyāhāra (withdrawal of the senses far from the external world); (6) Dhāraṇā (memory); (7) Dhyāna (meditation); (8) Samādhi (total concentration).

Yama and Niyama

Respect for all living creatures (this includes, for Hindus, charity and compassion in the widest sense with all the ethical rules involved) in order to regain the sāttvik state which is indispensable to Yogic practice.

Āsana

Āsana or the manner of sitting plays an important rôle in the performance of meditation, for different postures can have a strong influence over mental and physical functions.

Prāṇāyāma

Prāṇa is the life force, the very substance of our bodies. It is the basis of all thought and activity. With control of this life force or prāṇa control is also gained over all bodily organs. Through the exercise of prāṇāyāma complete domination over the emotions and over psychological disturbances is attained. Prāṇa is the active principle of the motor and sensory organs. If Yogins are held in India to be endowed with supra-natural faculties, this is partly on account of the practice of prāṇāyāma. But it must be understood that these extraordinary powers are not meant for display. The true Yogin reveals them to his most faithful disciples only.

According to Patañjali four distinct activities are to be seen in prāṇāyāma:

(a) recaka or expiration;
(b) pūraka or inspiration;
(c) kumbhaka or retention of the breath in the body;
(d) kevalakumbhaka, where the Yogin goes beyond the limits laid down.

In all these actions the Yogin must scrupulously perform his guru's instructions.

The other Yogāṅgas

Pratyāhāra: the Yogin withdraws his senses from the temptations of the outside world.

Dhāraṇā: a true conception of things.

Dhyāna: meditation in one of the āsanas. Without meditation nothing is possible.

Samādhi: this is the final stage which the Yogin reaches when he has attained complete spiritual fulfilment. Without samādhi it is impossible to know Truth. (Usha Chatterji, *op. cit.*)

The ancient doctrines of Yoga are broken up into the Haṭha Yoga (the āsanas and prāṇāyāma are its chief elements), Mantra Yoga, Laya Yoga, Rāja Yoga, Bhakti Yoga and Jñāna Yoga.

Only when he has practised the different disciplines common to all the Yogas does the Yogin begin to reap the fruit of dhyāna or "meditation" in the form of absolute concentration. Scholars trace the origins of the Laya Yoga in the Sāmaveda but its full explanation is to be found in the Chāndogya Upaniṣad.

In the Bhagavadgītā the Lord says:

1. "This unaltering Rule I declared to Vivasvat; Vivasvat declared it to Manu, and Manu told it to Ikshvāku.

2. "Thus was this Rule passed down in order, and kingly sages learned it; but by length of time, O affrighter of the foe, it has been lost here.

3. "Now is this ancient Rule declared by Me to thee, for that

thou art devoted to Me and friend to Me; for it is a most high mystery."[1]

THE HAṬHA YOGA

The purpose of the Haṭha Yoga is to destroy or transform all that which, in man, interferes with his union with the universal Being, whereby he may discover his own essence by means of certain rhythms connected with the regulation and control of respiration. It is a "Yoga of strength" which lays particular stress on physical exercises that even permit the adept to perform physiological feats that are normally beyond human capacity.

For this a fusion of two kinds of psychological current is necessary: prāṇa and apāna, absorption and rejection, a dualistic pattern from which differentiated existence arises.

The Haṭha Yoga is far from being only a specialized form of gymnastics and physical training, opposing, as it were, the spiritual training of the Rāja Yoga. "In fact, its use is based upon a principle of non-separation of body and mind, where both have as their common source of activity prāṇa or 'breath' and according to all authentic Haṭha Yogins mental training, in theory if not in practice, is the concomitant of physical training. It is, in any case, normal that psychological and somatic phenomena should be set to work together for their mutual benefit, especially since the Haṭhạ Yoga accords special importance to the action of the will upon the organs of the body." (Renou, *op. cit.*, p. 51.)

The Haṭha Yoga, then, is a form of training both psychological and physical based upon "breath". It is not restricted to any sect and can be practised in differing circumstances. But in India it is certainly of secondary importance in the life of the spirit.

THE MANTRA YOGA

Once he has obtained purification by the different disciplines of the Haṭha Yoga the Yogin must recite a series of mantras or

[1] *Bhagavadgītā*, IV, 1–3. Trans. L. D. Barnett.

"prayers" which make up the Mantra Yoga. To these is sometimes added a prolonged recitation of formulas which are a "declaration" of consciousness of the ātman.

THE LAYA YOGA

The aim of the Laya Yoga is to direct the mind upon the object of meditation. Once the Yogin has acquired breath-control he must achieve concentration of thought or dhāraṇā. This can be applied to any object, real or imaginary, exterior or interior, such as, for example, the tip of the nose or the space between the eyebrows. By this means he gains concentration of attention or ekāgratā.

THE RĀJA YOGA

The culmination of the preceding Yogas is the Rāja Yoga or royal Yoga which is "especially the state of union of Śiva and Śakti". In this Yoga mental concentration must be turned inwards like a light, so as to allow one to distinguish perfectly between real and unreal, finite and infinite, eternal and impermanent, until at length all identification of the self with what is not real, infinite and eternal disappears.

THE BHAKTI YOGA

The Bhakti Yoga is the Yoga of devotion, religion and love. It teaches the rules of love, for it is the science of the higher love; it teaches how to direct and use love and how to give it a new object, how to obtain from it the highest and most glorious result, which is the acquisition of spiritual felicity. The Bhakti Yoga does not say "abandon" but only "love, love the Most High" (Vivekananda, Bhakti Yoga).

"Whosoever is desired by this Ātman attains this Ātman and to him this Ātman is revealed. Whosoever is intensely loved by this Ātman will become the favourite of this Ātman. Thus, in order that the loved one might attain the Ātman, the Lord himself intervenes. For the Lord has said: 'I shall direct the will of those who offer Me constant attachment and adore Me with love and I shall show them the way to reach Me.' This continual remembrance is expressed by the word 'Bhakti'." (*Idem.*)

The Bhakti Yoga is a dualistic Yoga *par excellence* since its adept has no desire to merge into the consciousness of the Unity but, on the contrary, wishes to be conscious of the presence of God and to savour it intensely. What is essential in the Bhakti Yoga is to love God with all one's heart and soul and to strive towards him with the whole of one's being in order to be united with him.

THE JÑĀNA YOGA

The Jñāna Yoga is monist. The aim of asceticism is to reach Knowledge and gain access to noumenal truth. It is the most arduous way, reserved for an élite and in it the Yogin must go beyond the plane of Māyā.

To escape the consciousness of multiplicity is to escape from time, space and causality and to obtain Knowledge of the Absolute, of Brahman through knowledge of the ātman (ātmajñāna). To triumph over dualities is the first stage in relinquishing ignorance. Intellectual seeking must be constantly supplemented by a rigorous mental discipline. God can appear only when the ego ceases to count. Discrimination must be exercised the whole time and total renunciation of all attachment, however subtle, must be fully accepted. The Yogin can use as his criterion only his reason and intelligence; therefore Jñāna Yogins are few. Rāmaṇa Maharṣi, who died a few years ago, was one. He was completely inaccessible.

CHAPTER X

DEATH

Death in the Veda consists primarily in a funeral rite accompanied by chanted formulas intended to prevent the ghost of the dead man from returning to haunt the living. When the ceremony is over the dead reach the abode of Yama, the god of Death. They become "fathers" or pitṛs and gain immortality.

If, during the last existence, the rhythm of transmigration has not been broken and release attained, death appears only as a momentary disappearance from the earth. For one who "knows" and is "released", to die is to take the path of the gods from which there is no return. He thus breaks away from the fearful whirl of rebirths, since the subtle essence of his soul, his ātman, has been merged into the universal subtle essence that is Brahman. By identifying himself with it every mortal may obtain immortality.

1. So those . . . pass into the flame[1]; from the flame, into the day; from the day, into the half-month of the waxing moon; from the half-month of the waxing moon, into the six months during which the sun moves northward; [2] from those months, into the year; from the year, into the sun; from the sun, into the moon; from the moon, into the lightning. There there is a Person (puruṣa) who is non-human (amānava). He leads them on to Brahma. This is the way leading to the gods (Chāndogya Up. V. 10. i–ii. Trans. Hume).

This celestial journey of the soul, reserved for the brāhmans and mystics, is expressive of the way in which Indian thought tends towards unification and towards a return to primordial

[1] That is, into the flame of the cremation fire.

substances. Several parables in the Upaniṣads illustrate this: the parable of the honey, the unique liquor which the bees distil from the sap of all flowers, or the parable of the rivers and the ocean.

1. These rivers, my dear, flow, the eastern toward the east, the western toward the west. They go just from the ocean to the ocean. They become the ocean itself. As there they know not "I am this one," "I am that one"—[2] even so, indeed, my dear, all creatures here, though they have come forth from Being, know not "We have come forth from Being." Whatever they are in this world, whether tiger, or lion, or wolf, or boar, or worm, or fly, or gnat, or mosquito, that they become.

3. That which is the finest essence—this whole world has that as its soul. That is Reality. That is Ātman (Soul). That art thou, Śvetaketu.

(Chāndogya Up. VI. 10. i–iii. Trans. Hume.)

The path of the manes, used by the secular dead, that is by those who have striven in vain to free themselves from the cycle of saṁsāra or "transmigration", returns them to this world.

3. But those who in the village reverence a belief in sacrifice, merit, and almsgiving—they pass into the smoke[2]; from the smoke, into the night; from the night, into the latter half of the month; from the latter half of the month, into the six months during which the sun moves southward—these do not reach the year; [4] from those months, into the world of the fathers; from the world of the fathers, into space; from space, into the moon. That is King Soma. That is the food of the gods. The gods eat that.

5. After having remained in it as long as there is a residue [of their good works], then by that course by which they came they return again, just as they came, into space; from space, into wind. After having become wind, one becomes smoke. After having become smoke, he becomes mist.

6. After having become mist, he becomes cloud. After having become cloud, he rains down. They are born here as rice and barley, as herbs and trees, as sesame plants and beans. Thence, verily, indeed, it is difficult to emerge; for only if some one or other eats him as food and emits him as semen, does he develop further.

(Chāndogya Up. V. 10. iii–vi. Trans. Hume.)

[2] That is, into the smoke of the cremation fire.

A scrupulous justice presides over the end of every life. All receive retribution according to their works. Every effort represents a definitive gain for the indestructible soul, the emanation of the universe soul.

The Chāndogya Upaniṣad states:

1. Om! [The teacher should say:] "Now, what is here in this city of Brahma,[3] is an abode, a small lotus flower.[4] Within that is a small space. What is within that, should be searched out; that, assuredly, is what one should desire to understand."

2. If they [i.e. the pupils] should say to him: "This abode, the small lotus-flower that is here in this city of Brahma, and the small space within that—what is there there which should be searched out, which assuredly one should desire to understand?" [3] he should say: "As far, verily, as this world-space (ayam ākāśa) extends, so far extends the space within the heart. Within it, indeed, are contained both heaven and earth, both fire and wind, both sun and moon, lightning and the stars, both what one possesses here and what one does not possess; everything here is contained within it."

4. If they should say to him: "If within this city of Brahma is contained everything here, all beings as well as all desires, when old age overtakes it or it perishes, what is left over therefrom?" [5] he should say: "That does not grow old with one's old age; it is not slain with one's murder. That[5] is the real city of Brahma. In it desires are contained. That is the Soul (Ātman), free from evil, ageless, deathless, sorrowless, hungerless, thirstless, whose desire is the Real, whose conception is the Real.

"For, just as here on earth human beings follow along in subjection to command; of whatever object they are desirous, whether a realm or a part of a field, upon that they live dependent—

6. "As here on earth the world which is won by work (karma-jita loka) becomes destroyed; even so there the world which is won by merit (puṇya-jita loka) becomes destroyed.

"Those who go hence without here having found the Soul (Ātman) and those real desires (satya kāma)—for them in all the worlds there is no freedom. But those who go hence having found here the Soul and those real desires—for them in all worlds there is freedom."

[3] Explained by Śaṅkara as "the body."
[4] Explained by Śaṅkara as "the heart."
[5] And not the body.

The idea of the three worlds frequently occurs in the Upaniṣads in the context of death. There is the world here below, the upper world and an intermediate stage between the two which is a state of slumber extending between consciousness and unconsciousness. The spirit wanders with its dreams like a great fish between the shores of the two worlds. Dreams give glimpses of the after life through fleeting visits which precede definitive absorption into, and communion with, Brahman.

Carrying with him his knowledge and actions mortal man embarks upon a new existence. If he is a sage, devoid of all desire, his ātman shakes off the carnal body and sheds "non-being" as "a snake sheds its old skin and draws itself together for a new plunge forward".

Souls, though pure in their essence, lose the appearance of purity through their temporary individual limitations. These create the illusion known as māyā which is caused by the world of "names and forms". Each individual soul strives to break through its limitations by an infinite expansion of the personality and thereby to attain knowledge. This oblivion of the self or supreme identification is Beatitude. It is like a drop of pure water falling into pure water. This soul then follows "the path of the gods to reach the Paradise it longs for and which corresponds to its own spiritual level, for paradises are 'states of consciousness' ". The impure soul is judged by Yama, whose weight creates a deficit in the scales, and is sent to hell where punishment is meted out to it according to the sins it has committed. But neither paradise nor hell is eternal. The last thought, upon the very threshold of death, can decide the fate of the soul. Death concerns the body only; hence the funeral liturgy of the Hindu religion is addressed to the dead man himself, to his soul as freed from the body: "Depart, depart by the ancient paths of our ancestors. Thou shalt see Yama and Varuṇa, the two kings who desire the funeral offering. Go thou and live in the highest heaven with the Fathers, with Yama and with thine offerings."

At death the man "who does not know" returns into his fluid body which is the seed of his future body. Only the physical envelope, the fleshly body dies. There can be neither birth nor death for the psychological faculties that make up man's second envelope or subtle body.

When life ends cremation hastens the dissolution process of the physical remains. Each element within the body returns to its source. While the fire is consuming the corpse the celebrant says in the ritual: "Let thine eye go to the sun, thy breath into the wind. Go to heaven or to earth as the law commands; into the waters if such is thy destiny; or into the plants with thy bodily parts" (Rigveda, X. 16. iii).

According to Indian beliefs imponderable elements support the freed soul which, since it is deprived of its physical organs, cannot at first be conscious of its passage from one life to another. But it is certainly the same soul which goes through a whole series of existences: dreamless sleep does not prevent the sleeper from being the same as the man who awakes afterwards. Two consecutive lives, divided by an absorption into Brahman, are like two successive vigils separated by a night with or without dreams, for is not dreamless sleep a brief absorption into Brahman, according to the Vedic texts?

The soul cannot die as the body does. The mirage of life on earth creates an illusion for the human mind which believes in their reality. It forgets that the "golden thread', the infallible guide towards that Unity which will free it from its temporary isolation, from its fleshly prison, is the only reality here on earth.

Much light is thrown upon death in the Kaṭha Upaniṣad where it is depicted in the full orthodoxy of Vedic belief. This Upaniṣad is an account of a descent into hell and it is made the more mysterious by the rite of fire.

Naciketas, a young Brāhman, is sent, in spite of his religious zeal, into the other world by his father who has given way to a sudden fit of anger. He proceeds to the land of the dead. Yama, the god of Death (since he was the first to die), who is busy elsewhere, does not greet his arrival with the ceremony which the young man's caste demands. Now, the laws of hospitality are regarded as one of the greatest traditions of India, even in the kingdom of the Shades. Embarrassed by his own negligence towards a guest of quality, Yama offers to grant Naciketas three wishes.

The young man's first wish is to return to his father. His second is to possess the secret of the fire rite by which death is avoided. Yama agrees to grant the first two wishes but draws back amazed before the Brāhman's third.

> Naciketas asks Yama: "What is death?"
> This doubt that there is in regard to a man deceased:
> "He exists," say some; "He exists not," say others—
> This would I know, instructed by thee!
> Of the boons this is boon the third.
> [Death:]
> Even the gods had doubt as to this of yore!
> For truly, it is not easily to be understood. Subtile is this matter (dharma).
> Another boon, O Naciketas, choose!
> Press me not! Give up this one for me!

The young Brāhman refuses to give way and insists on his question. Yama does not want to give away his secret and tries to make him forget this unfortunate wish by tempting him with the greatest of human satisfactions.

The riches of this mortal world, skilfully enumerated by Yama, leave Naciketas untouched. He casts them aside as fleeting and gravely asks the god of Death:

> This thing whereon they doubt, O Death:
> What there is in the great passing-on—tell us that!
> This boon, that has entered into the hidden—
> No other than that does Naciketas choose.

The problem has been stated, the ritual left behind; now speculation begins.

Yama explains to the young man that on earth men are led by desires, the wise man preferring the highest good, the foolish man what is most pleasant.

The idea of escaping from the cycle of pain which is transmigration cannot enter the mind of those who believe this world to be the only one and they remain in its power. Knowledge of the Absolute remains inaccessible to most beings, Yama continues, for the Absolute is incomparably more subtle than any measurable subtlety. And he congratulates Naciketas on his disdain for might and vainglory and on his control over body and mind. This spiritual elevation makes him worthy to question the god of Death, who now willingly answers him who, in order to contemplate Death alone, has left behind him grief and joy without turning back.

Treating Naciketas as "a dwelling open for Brahman" he reveals to him the secret word.

> The word which all the Vedas rehearse,
> And which all austerities proclaim,
> Desiring which men live the life of religious studentship (brahma-carya)—
> That word to thee I briefly declare.
> That is Om!
> That syllable, truly, indeed, is Brahma!
> That syllable indeed is the supreme!
> Unborn, constant, eternal, primeval, this one
> Is not slain when the body is slain.
> If the slayer think to slay,
> If the slain think himself slain,
> Both these understand not.
> This one slays not, nor is slain.
> ....
> Him who is the bodiless among bodies,
> Stable among the unstable,
> The great, all-pervading Soul (Ātman)—
> On recognizing Him, the wise man sorrows not.
> This Soul (Ātman) is not to be obtained by instruction,
> Nor by intellect, nor by much learning.
> He is to be obtained only by the one whom He chooses;
> To such a one that Soul (Ātman) reveals his own person (tanūm svām).

According to the Kaṭha Upaniṣad Grace, which Śaṁkara in his turn was to expound later in the Vedānta, intervenes in the choice of the blessed when they discover the divine nature of their ātman.

The third part of the Upaniṣad compares the ātman to the possessor of a chariot represented by the body. The senses are the horses and the objects of sense are the road to be travelled.

The god of Death teaches the absolute necessity of controlling all thoughts and desires.

> He, however, who has not understanding,
> Who is unmindful and ever impure,
> Reaches not the goal,
> But goes on to transmigration (saṁsāra).
> He, however, who has understanding,
> Who is mindful and ever pure,
> Reaches the goal
> From which he is born no more.

Yama concludes that the only way of escaping death is to vanquish it. To do so the self must be transcended, must be made the equal of the divine ātman, "smaller than a grain of millet and greater than the earth and sky", of this ātman which each carries within him in the depths of his heart. By transcending himself man passes beyond death. From the funeral ceremony—death is no more than a rite in the Veda—there has grown, like the oak from the acorn, a spirituality which makes men like to gods.

Here are the last lines of the Kaṭha Upaniṣad:

> Arise ye! Awake ye!
> Obtain your boons[6] and understand them!
> A sharpened edge of a razor, hard to traverse,
> A difficult path is this—poets (kavi) declare!
> Without beginning, without end, higher than the great, stable—
> By discerning That, one is liberated from the mouth of death.
> The Naciketas tale,
> Death's immortal teaching—
> By declaring and hearing this, a wise man
> Is magnified in the Brahma-world.
> If one recites this supreme secret
> In an assembly of Brahmans,
> Or at a time of the ceremony for the dead, devoutly—
> That makes for immortality!
> —That makes for immortality!

(From the Kaṭha Upaniṣad: I. 20, 21, 29. II. 15, 16, 18c, 19, 22, 23. III. 7, 8, 14, 15c–d, 16, 17. Trans. Hume, *The Thirteen Principal Upanishads.*)

[6] The commentators interpret "boons" as referring to "teachers". But the word may imply "answers to your questions".

CHAPTER XI

THE SECTS

When a population is as vast as that of India, it is natural that, during the course of thousands of years, where a religion has had an unhindered evolution, divergences in doctrine and, therefore, sects should arise. Some die out, more are formed while yet others again are found to persist.

"The sects", says L. Renou, "have obviously never affected all adepts. Some of them are only tiny groups and, even in the case of the most important, adherence must often have been more nominal than real."

The various sects derive from the teachings of the Veda through the Upaniṣads, the Sāṁkhya or the Vedānta and are but different aspects of one and the same truth.

The Hindus do not restrict the possible number of divine incarnations or Avatars. God is immortal, infinite, ageless. He can appear under different aspects. By taking on fresh guises the incarnate gods awaken and intensify the devotion of believers.

In the Bhagavadgītā Kṛṣṇa declares: 7. "For whensoever the Law fails and lawlessness uprises, O thou of Bharata's race, then do I bring Myself to bodied birth.

8. "To guard the righteous, to destroy evildoers, to establish the Law, I come into birth age after age" (Bhagavadgītā IV. Trans. L. D. Barnett).

Sects are the traditional outcome when the driving force of a divine incarnation, a master or a saint, manifests itself in the Sanātana Dharma. New cults are added to the old ones without mutual harm or strife and enjoying complete internal freedom. Whenever any attempt at religious amalgamation or syncretism is made it will always proceed in a spirit of a deep awareness of identity of purpose, even though the ways followed may differ.

Śaṁkarācārya has said: "The unity of the supreme God is well illustrated in this explanation of the Vedas: Truth is One, but wise men give it many names. These names, which are honoured and worshipped by different religions, are but symbols which enable finite minds to grasp the Infinite. The divinities for which they stand are but so many facets of the ineffable reality that is One."

Moreover, "revelation" does not stop but continues perpetually for those who know how to "listen" to God and whom God chooses.

In the Gītā Kṛṣṇa speaks to Arjuna as follows:—". . . Thou art devoted to Me and friend to Me . . ." (IV. 3). "There is no bound to My divine powers . . ." (X. 40). "On these, who are ever under the Rule, worshipping Me with love, I bestow the Rule of Understanding, whereby they come to Me" (X. 10). (Bhagavadgītā, trans., L. D. Barnett.)

The aim of a new sect or religion is generally to react against an excess, to return to a purer form or to evolve in a particular direction held to be necessary.

It is said that the Buddha came so that certain errors might be corrected. Perhaps it was because the caste system had grown too rigid or that the ritual was being too literally interpreted. The Buddha is considered in India as one of the greatest sages and spiritual teachers of mankind. Buddhism took root in ancient times; it grew as a divergent branch upon the trunk of the Veda. After dominating India for several centuries it disappeared completely, only to develop elsewhere. Jainism, so akin to Buddhism, spread much less and remained static. These different religions certainly influenced each other. But the two latter are not relevant to this study since they did not preserve the orthodoxy of the Veda.

The cults of Viṣṇu, Śiva and the Śakti form the most important religious groups in India. These cults neither oppose nor contradict each other. They are a means and not an end in themselves, for that would necessarily lead to spiritual stagnation. Their aims are identical: the union of all beings with the supreme Being; this is the ultimate striving of the Hindu religion.

VAIṢṆAVISM

Vaiṣṇavism is the worship of Viṣṇu incarnate as Kṛṣṇa, Rāma and his other "avatars". In the Rigveda Viṣṇu was the sun, the symbol of all activity (viṣ means "to be active"). "It is said that Viṣṇu is the god of Time, Space and Life. It is also said that he is the god of Joy and that his footsteps are impregnated with infinite sweetness and felicity."

In the Rigveda Varuṇa was the chief of the Ādityas; it is an easy step to assimilate him with Viṣṇu with whom he was associated. In the same way Bhaga, the god of fertility in the Rigveda, is also identified with Viṣṇu. There is little doubt that Bhaga or Viṣṇu, the central figure of the Bhāgavatas, was an important stage in the early development of the cult of Viṣṇu from which Vaiṣṇavism sprang.

Bhakti or "devotion" lies at the core of Vaiṣṇavism. It is that love of human beings for the divine in which every religion is steeped but none more than the Indian religion known as Vaiṣṇavism. Bhakti is that true quest for the supreme Being which begins with the love of God and ends in complete spiritual fulfilment. For the Vaiṣṇava the Bhakti Yoga is the chief road to spiritual release. Vaiṣṇavas are pure mystics and place devotion on a higher level than any other form of religious exercise: "By devotion he recognizes in verity who and what I am; then, knowing Me in verity, he speedily enters into Me." "He who serves Me with unswerving rule of devotion becomes by passage beyond the Moods fit for Brahmahood" (Bhagavadgītā, XVIII. 55 and XIV. 26. Trans. L. D. Barnett). The Gītā also says: "God is the immutable centre of infinite mobility". For the adept Kṛṣṇa is the symbol of this.

The "intuitive knowledge" of which the Vaiṣṇava mystics speak may be defined as follows. When the soul, whose most natural activity is to contribute to the beatific exercises of Kṛṣṇa in heaven, is disturbed under the influence of māyā, the spirit escapes and attaches itself to objects of the phenomenal world, though it will always have a tendency (ātmapreraṇa) to revert to its original state. The theological name of this tendency is svarūpannvandhita. The original state becomes permanent when devotion and practice are constant. That is the intuitive vision of the Vaiṣṇava mystics.

The Pāñcarātra sect

Pāñcarātra is the name given to a Vaiṣṇava doctrine of Southern India. "The meaning of this term still eludes scholars." A plausible interpretation of this term does, however, exist which would connect it with certain vows formulated five times (pañca = "five") a year, after the analogy of the seasons (rātra).[1]

In the opinion of Louis Renou the Pāñcarātras seem, in ancient times, to have been the repository of the specifically Vaiṣṇava canon, known under the generic title of Saṁhitās.

The theology of the Pāñcarātras postulates a supreme personal brahman, at once immanent and transcendental, who reveals himself in the form of Viṣṇu, Vāsudeva and Nārāyaṇa. The universe is conceived of as the product of a Śakti or "motive force" inherent in this supreme principle. The Śrīvaiṣṇava movement (the cult of Viṣṇu with his spouse) is an offshoot of the Pāñcarātra which took root in the Tamil country. "The first masters of the Śrīvaiṣṇava sect were the Alvārs who crystallized the conception of devotional faith in its Vaiṣṇava form and composed a popular body of hymns and narrative literature." (Renou, *Hindouisme*, p. 99.)

The Bhāgavata sect

The doctrines of the Bhāgavatas are an expression of Hinduism based essentially upon the grace which God pours out for human kind and upon belief in the divine incarnations. The Bhāgavatas or "Devotees of the Blessed One" have, for their sacred texts, the Bhāgavata Purāṇa and the Viṣṇu Purāṇa. They are entirely given over to religious love.

[1] U. Chatterji, *op. cit.*

"The Vaiṣṇava is primarily a devotionalist. Even when he finds difficulty in concentration he still sees himself as God and always remains conscious of the eternal reality. His actions and thoughts towards God are always of an individual character and bear analogy with those of a mother towards her son, a husband towards his wife or a fiancée towards her lover. Mystical union with the supreme Being is a personal experience which binds together the human and divine."[2]

The Bhāgavata Purāṇa and the Viṣṇu Purāṇa were very popular at the Gupta period (4th–6th centuries). It was the Gupta kings who adopted the name of Bhāgavatas and gave new impetus to the writing of the Purāṇas. They constructed temples in honour of Viṣṇu in many places. They drew into this cult the dynasties of Southern and Northern India and of the Deccan. Strengthened by the Rajput kings, the influence of this cult spread to the whole of India.

The Rāmānuja sect

The name of Rāmānuja, who was born in 1017 near Madras and died in 1137, is of special relevance to Vaiṣṇavism. Rāmānuja dedicated himself entirely to devotion, charity and sanctity and made a particular study of the Prabandha and the esoteric doctrine of the Nārāyaṇīya. He evolved a philosophy of qualified monism called Viśiṣṭādvaita and is the most eminent of Vaiṣṇava philosophers. "He instituted a form of Vedānta based on the concept of the 'qualified brahman', that is to say, of a personal God endowed with attributes and embracing souls and matter." (Renou, *Hindouisme*, p. 99.)

The Vedārthasaṁgraha, one of his first works, consists in a highly detailed analysis of the Upaniṣads. Rāmānuja, who was a great popularizer of Vaiṣṇavism, accepted non-Brāhmans among his disciples and treated them in all things exactly like the others except that they were not allowed to wear the sacred thread or to study the Veda. His learned works were of considerable importance as was the rôle he played in social reforms. The

[2] Usha Chatterji, *op. cit.*, pp. 32, 33.

Rāmānujas (followers of Rāmānuja) are numerous to this day in Tamil regions and their literature is as abundant in Sanskrit as in Tamil.

The sect of the Nīmānandins or Nimbārkas

This sect claims to follow Nimbārka who professed a "non-dualist dualism", a doctrine which continued that of the astronomer Bhāskara and aimed at establishing a link between the Absolute and multiple phenomena.

The Mādhva sect

"Founded in the thirteenth century by Mādhva, otherwise known as Ānandatīrtha, a Kanarese sage, this sect preaches a salvation attainable by immediate and intuitive knowledge of the divinity. On its speculative side it remains akin to that of the Rāmānujas. . . . Its philosophical stand is total dualism—a confrontation of the omnipresent Viṣṇu and, on the other hand, souls and matter. Its ascetics are drawn from Śaṁkaran orders. The literature (mainly in Sanskrit) is fairly considerable. This doctrine continues even at the present day in the South, though it is favoured more by the intellectual classes than in the popular strata of society" (L. Renou, *op. cit.*, p. 101).

The sect of the Rāmānandins or Rāmāvants

The Rāmānandin sect hold Rāmānanda to be their master. Its adherents worship Viṣṇu under the form of Rāma. A body of monks, the vairāgins, was founded by this sect. Rāmānanda, who was of Śrīvaiṣṇava loyalties, was little concerned with philosophy but kept as basic to his doctrine the Śrīvaiṣṇava tenets. This is the first sect to have accorded Rāma the position of supreme God.

The Vallabha sect

The Vallabha sect was founded in the fifteenth century by a Telugu sage "whose philosophical outlook was that of a 'pure' non-dualism in which the world is the product of an internal transformation of the Absolute. Vallabha evolved a theory of devotionalism and postulated a double approach to release, the so-called way of the 'frontier' which demands a personal effort and the way of the 'blossoming' which depends entirely upon divine grace" (Renou, *op. cit.*, p. 102).

The Caitanya sect

In the fifteenth century Caitanya became the central figure of medieval Vaiṣṇavism and his is the greatest name associated with that sect. He was born in Bengal in 1485 and he died in 1533. He was a true apostle and visionary and revived the flagging ardour of believers by the strength of his own at an age when India was afflicted and ravaged by Muslim invaders. Few saints have received in their own lifetime as many marks of respect and devotion as Caitanya. He was considered an incarnation of Viṣṇu on account of the extraordinary power he radiated. Six of his disciples, the Gosvāmins, codified in Sanskrit every aspect of his doctrine and expounded in its entirety the cult of Kṛṣṇa in association with Rādhā.

"The descendants of the Gosvāmins are heads of monasteries and temples. Their ritual involves a chanted 'glorification' in Bengali or Hindi and numerous practices representing what Vaiṣṇavism holds to be materially most evolved" (Renou, *op. cit.*, p. 102).

The sect of the Kabīrpanthīs

The sect of the Kabīrpanthīs was founded by Kabīr, a disciple of Rāmānanda. Kabīr, a Hindu ascetic with a Muslim name, strove to reconcile Hinduism and Islam on the basis of a non-figurative monotheism. The numerous verses of Kabīr are used as the canonical literature of this sect.

The Sikhs

This group was founded by Nānak (1486–1538), himself a disciple of Kabīr. The Sikhs, moreover, have much in common with the Muslims and live chiefly in Central and Northern

India. Nānak was a Panjābi from the region of Lahore. He believed in the Vedānta, in devotionalism and in the cult of the guru. The Sikh canon is called the "Noble Book". This sect is, to the present day, active in the Panjāb. The holy city of the Sikhs is Amritsar where the "Golden Temple" stands,

The sect of the Dādūpanthīs

The Dādūpanthīs are the disciples of Dādū (seventeenth century) and have much in common with the sects already described.

The hymns of the Vaiṣṇavas are called kīrtans or sometimes bhajans. They are sung in temples, in the home and at religious concourses. For the Hindu a special virtue resides in these hymns. In the event of some disaster or an epidemic, the Vaiṣṇavas immediately start singing their Harikīrtans. If there is an outbreak of cholera or smallpox in some village, a group of singers assembles and for a whole week they chant in relays. This is known as the Aṣṭaprahar Harinām. (Usha Chatterji, *op. cit.*) But this custom is also followed without any practical purpose for love of Kṛṣṇa alone. It takes place at nightfall under a tree or in some other propitious place. When a death occurs, kīrtans are always sung in the bereaved household during the funeral ceremony.

With care it is always possible to pick out a genuine Vaiṣṇava in a crowd, for most often he will be found dressed in orange or white with a vaiṣṇava rosary in his hand. Hindus show their sectarian loyalties in various ways, either by the cut of their hair or by coloured marks on the forehead. The Vaiṣṇava paints red or white vertical lines on his forehead or red, black or white spots between the eyebrows.

ŚAIVISM

Śaivism is the religion of those who see in Śiva the manifestation of the supreme Being. In their view Śiva is in everyone. Śaivism dates from the earliest time of Indian history and is one of the principal forms of the Hindu religion. The Śaivite faithful understand and interpret Śiva in many fashions, depending on their metaphysical leanings. According to some he is a divinity whose antiquity and greatness can scarcely be rivalled. Others see him as the symbol of a philosophy. Others again see him as God himself. So it happens that every Hindu (and in particular the Śaiva) looks upon the Lord Śiva as his own character and degree of spiritual development allow.

> Be it in the Vedas, the Upaniṣads or the Purāṇas, the Lord Śiva is always referred to with great reverence as well as under different names. The conception of Śiva is not simply that of a godhead whose powers have become concentrated in a single figure dominating a certain period of Indian history. Śiva is identified with the Eternal and the All-powerful; he is the Primal Soul and the Great Soul from which uncounted other souls have sprung. Śiva is beauty, Śiva is all, he is everywhere. There is no life, no motion and no rhythm without Śiva, for he is the Cosmos itself. (Usha Chatterji, *La danse hindoue*.)

In the Rigveda Śiva is often called Rudra, "The lord of songs and of sacrifices, who remedies and heals, is brilliant as the sun, the best and most generous of the gods, who grants prosperity and welfare. . . ." In the Yajurveda he is Tryambaka "with three eyes, a blue neck . . . Tryambaka, the sweet-scented".

The compilation of the Purāṇas was not without its inspiration and this body of literature is rich in imagery and colour. In the course of its philosophical narrations we are shown Śiva in his aspect of "taker" (Hara) and of "the well-omened" (Śaṁkara).

In the Upaniṣads Śiva thus proclaims his greatness:

"I existed before all else and I exist now and shall exist hereafter. No other transcends me. I am eternal and not eternal, discernible and not discernible. I am Brahmā and I am not Brahmā."

"He is without beginning, middle or end. He is unique, the omnipresent lord, three-eyed, with a blue neck. He is the tranquil one. . . ."

In the Dvāpara yuga (which was that of the Mahābhārata) Śiva was accorded the highest honours by Kṛṣṇa and Viṣṇu and became all-powerful. Then he was One, Being, Non-being, the Infinite and the Indivisible and the trinity was then no more than different manifestations of the sole principle.

THE SUPREME CONCEPT IN ITS MANIFESTATION

In the Hindu trinity Śiva is the lord of destruction, for without it creation cannot be. On the one hand he is identified with Time and Death in their destructive functions; on the other he restores and is the "beneficent one" as his names of Śiva, Śaṁbhu and Śaṁkara indicate. He has two further major functions. (Innumerable other names are used for him as well in less important contexts.) He is, first of all, the Lord of Destruction. Secondly he is the Eternal Yogin and thirdly the Bestower of Gifts. The concept of Śiva in his aspect as Naṭarāja is automatically linked with that of his aspect as Lord of Destruction and symbolizes the unity of created and uncreated things.

The dance of Śiva, called the dance of Nadanta, is fraught with meaning. It was so beautiful that one of the faithful asked the god to repeat it. He consented and Śiva Naṭarāja danced once again in the temple of Cidambaram which subsequently remained associated with that event. The central theme of the dance is the visual representation of the five main activities of the master, the Pañcakṛtya. These activities are also sometimes separately attributed to Brahmā, Viṣṇu, Rudra, Maheśvara and Sadāśiva (the "ever-benevolent"), the last three names being those of Śiva, the One and Only.

The five activities (the Pañcakṛtya) are:

1. Sṛṣṭi: creation and evolution.
2. Sthiti: maintaining and preserving.
3. Saṁhāra: destruction and evolution.
4. Tirobhava: the incarnation of souls.
5. Anugraha: liberation from the karmic cycle.

The temple of Cidambaram symbolizes the centre of the universe or rather the centre of our hearts. The mystic meaning of this dance is that the Supreme is within us and not outside of us. The dance is enacted in our very hearts. Śiva, being primarily Naṭarāja, dances the total destruction of the universe. He represents man's annihilation of his ego, of his illusions and disillusions. He is the symbol of the complete self-destruction which, for the Hindu mind, includes by implication the power of reproduction and by it all that has been dissolved is perpetually recreated. In this function Śiva is Iśvara, the supreme God and Mahādeva, the great God.

The followers of Śiva are mostly disciples of the Vedānta upon which Śaivism is based. Outward forms are necessary to incarnate souls in order that they may conceive in a certain measure that which is Inconceivable but outward forms cannot imprison the Infinite. Those who understand that they do not need a temple to meditate can meditate just as well in the snow, in a cave, a cellar, a shack or a forest.

Amongst the sects connected with the cult of Śiva the following may be mentioned.

The Kāpālikas

The Kāpālikas (who derive their name from the title Śiva kapālin = "bearer of human skulls") are a group of ascetics with extremist tendencies whose chief religious practices are singing and dancing. Their philosophy lies in reducing the diversity of creation to two elements: the Lord (pati), cause and creator (kartṛ) of all that "is", and, secondly, the creation (kārya) that emanates from him.

The Gorakhnāthīs (or Kāṇphaṭayogins, "yogins with split ears"), who venerate their master Gorakhnāth, a native of eastern Bengal, are a somewhat scattered group, consisting of a school of Yoga (Haṭha Yoga), and are found chiefly in northern India.

The Pāśupatas

The Pāśupatas or "adepts of Śiva" are Yogins who attain mystical ecstasy by means of somewhat violent practices. Their doctrine is based upon a dualism between souls and Śiva whose body is "made of energy".

"The other sects have as their canon, directly or indirectly, the sacred texts known as Āgamas. Their ritual and doctrine resemble those of Tantrism. The soul is conceived of as being imprisoned by the 'triple chain' or soiled by the 'triple taint' (ignorance, karman, māyā) and obtains release through the grace of the Master" (Renou, *op. cit.*, p. 96).

The Śaivism of Kashmir

This system, with its threefold teaching known under the name of Trika, is dominated by the tenth-century figure of Abhinavagupta and based on an elaborate non-dualism. The philosophy of this purely speculative movement rests on the objectivization of the thought of Śiva from which the world is evolved. This process occurs through the evolution of the thirty-six elements (tattvas). Release is obtained by means of "recognition"—the soul regains consciousness of the truths relevant to its real state, which truths had been obscured by māya or "illusion".

The Vīraśaivas

The Vīraśaivas or Liṅgāyats, "bearers of the liṅga", arose as a group in about the twelfth century in the southern Maratha country under the leadership of Basava. This sect rejects the Veda, caste and images; it seeks to emancipate women, while at the same time retaining private rites and sacraments. It is a non-dualism qualified by a śakti and in it souls and matter are realities which the śakti engenders. "The sect is directed by wandering monks known as jaṅgamas or 'travelling liṅgas'." They possess a considerable body of learned texts.

Śāktism: the Śāktas

The cult of the goddess Durgā is closely connected with Śaivism. It consists of a belief in śakti or "divine energy". This cult goes back to the Veda and while preserving the worship of Śiva it concentrates its attention on the cult of the feminine form of the god, that is, of the śakti or "divine energy". Śāktism, like

Vaiṣṇavism and Śaivism, is one of the sects which attracts the greatest number of adepts. Śāktism possesses a theology and a cult of which the Tantras constitute an important body of literature.

The basic texts of the Śākta cult are the Devī Bhāgavata Purāṇa and the Caṇḍī Māhātmya. The centre of these sects used to be in Bengal. A recent literature of a śākta type concerns the adoration of a divine Mother with an emotional devotionalism of the kind paid to Kṛṣṇa. This tendency was illustrated in the eighteenth century by certain Bengali poets (the poetry of Bharatacandra and Rāmprasad Sen).

The speculative doctrines of Śaivism conclude, as a whole, in a process of identification of the individual with the supreme Being. This is what makes Śaivism tend towards Tantrism and towards Yoga.

Tantrism

Tantrism or the religion of the Tantras is an autonomous development of Yoga which takes its initial direction from original physiological and cosmogonic constructs. The essential act of initiation is the receiving of the mantra by the pupil from his spiritual master or guru.

CHAPTER XII

THE CASTES

The social structure of India is based on the caste system, a system adopted by almost all human societies at the beginning of their evolution.

Perhaps other causes, difficult to estimate at the present time, have also contributed to this social division. To the necessity for a division of labour and individual tasks was added the ethnic reason of preserving the race against the impurity of intermarriage and this demanded a certain rigidity in the social framework. But it is likely that at the Vedic period, the caste system was more flexible and became rigid only later.

Most Europeans have no understanding of the caste system which is defined as an institution of primordial importance in the Laws of Manu. It allows each individual to be allotted that function in society for which his own nature best equips him. In this system lies the basis of an hierarchic organization with its great organized religious and administrative bodies which represent in four castes the whole of the Indian people.

THE BRĀHMANS

The first caste (varṇa, jāti), that of the Brāhmans, is the only truly religious one. It possesses the spiritual authority, although the other castes participate in varying degrees in sacred rites. The members of the first three classes, who are "twice-born" (dvija), are entitled at the age of twelve to the Initiation or Upanayana, which consecrates the child's entry into the Brāhmanic community and involves his investiture with the sacred thread. The Brāhman, however, has the right to a superior thread.

The Laws of Manu declare that "the very birth of a Brāhman is the eternal incarnation of the Law". This highly civilized class is largely made up of intellectuals, philosophers and writers whose work it is to study sacred texts, laws and the technical works. The Brāhman's duty is to teach the Veda and everything that is in any way of a priestly nature. They hold priestly office and it is necessary to be "born" a priest by "sacrificing" for others. They also receive the gifts of the faithful. But since they are bound to the strict observance of rites and ceremonies according to rigorously specified rules and since this absorbs a great part of their time, they are dispensed from any preoccupation with securing material goods. They are therefore supported by the state.

The Brāhmans stand at the top of the social hierarchy and have many privileges. Whenever a Brāhman appeared at Court, the sovereign would prostrate himself at his feet with the greatest show of respect on account of his superior caste and also because "wisdom" was held in the highest possible esteem.

Caste was the reward for merit before it became the automatic consequence of birth. Amongst the obligations incumbent upon the Brāhman is the ritual one of bathing twice a day in flowing water. The Brāhman must be a vegetarian and must wear the sacred thread symbolizing his caste.

Each day, after performing certain ceremonies, Brāhmans were required to meditate upon a particular mantra, that is, upon a stanza from a hymn. These mantras, when pronounced in accordance with the rules, were held to be endowed with an esoteric quality. The hymns of the Vedas are composed of mantras, the most important of which is that called the "Gāyatrī"; this is addressed to the sun and by Hindu tradition may be pronounced by the first three castes only.

"In Vedic times a mleccha, that is, a non-Aryan, could become a Brāhman. The caste was open to all and it was merely necessary to possess the requisite qualifications. Later, the three castes became separated by watertight partitions and it was impossible to pass from one to the other." (Swāmi Siddheśvarānanda, *Aspects de la philosophie védantique.*)

Upon becoming a monk (saṁnyāsin) a man is automatically freed from his social condition, he discards the sacred thread and is no longer bound to the thrice daily ritual repetition of the sacred "gāyatrī" symbolic of Brāhmanic initiation. The saṁnyāsin is above the four castes whereas the pariahs are below them.

THE KṢATRIYAS

The Kṣatriya class is the warrior caste whose task it is to defend the right, to protect the weak and to use force whenever it is legitimately justified.

Sovereigns are recruited from the Kṣatriya sect. The king, who is the embodiment of the Kṣatriyas, is an emanation of the divinity, a "god in human form" as Manu says (Renou), "and the great royal ceremonies had, even in post-Vedic India, the character of religious feasts. These are the only survivals of the ancient solemn cult offered to the great divinities."

The rôle of the Kṣatriya class, representing the nobility, lies in embodying honour by remaining faithful to one's word until death. The Kṣatriyas, while fulfilling as many duties as the Brāhmans, though of a rather different kind, yet owe respect to the Brāhmans. Of this warrior caste only the Rajputs survive. The remainder of the caste has turned to clerical professions and constitutes a sort of middle class.

THE VAIŚYAS

The function of the third or Vaiśya class is to administer and deal in material goods of every description. The Vaiśyas assumed the internal and foreign trade of India and it is thanks to them that textiles, precious stones and other products and foodstuffs were sold in foreign markets. This social class, the one which carries the most weight, corresponds to the middle class. Its chief activities are agriculture, the rearing of livestock and industry.

THE ŚŪDRAS

The dharma or duty of this last caste is to serve the three others to the best of its ability by manual labour (of which certain types are reserved to the "untouchables"). But the tasks which fall to the lot of the Śūdras could quite well be performed by Hindus of the other three castes.

The Śūdras have never been slaves. They were free to carry on or to leave their work and function. Their class forms the main body of the population and includes every kind of worker: servants, gardeners, shepherds, artisans, workmen and so forth.

They are not allowed to learn the Veda but may study the Itihāsas (the great epic cycle) and the Purāṇas.

These four great castes are themselves subdivided into innumerable subcastes and it could almost be said that there are thousands of them in India.

THE PARIAHS

The Pariahs are those that belong to no caste at all, nor are they admitted amongst the saṁnyāsins. They are called "untouchables" or "outcasts" and nothing is known of their precise origin, although the Laws of Manu state this: "Illicit marriages between people of different castes, marriages contrary to rule, omission of the prescribed ceremonies, these are the origin of the impure classes."

Since they are not bound by the strict rules which every caste must observe, the Pariahs enjoy, in some ways, a much greater freedom in spite of the prohibitions which affect them in other matters. Gandhi made himself their champion and obtained that some of India's great temples should be opened to them. "Expulsion from the caste represents a sort of excommunication and most caste rules are based upon the idea of segregation which follows easily from the religious importance given to purity and impurity" (Renou).

The "untouchables", who are a minority, have their own laws and live outside the community. Among them are butchers, tanners, gravediggers and sweepers. "The restrictions from which they suffer involve much less than is generally supposed" (Herbert, *op. cit.*). But India has known "untouchables" amongst its great saints—Nanda, Ravidāsa, Colamela and Haridāsa. "The Laws of Manu themselves admit that in certain castes Pariahs of the lowest and most degraded groups may directly obtain supreme bliss" (*ibid.*, p. 194).

CHAPTER XIII

THE TEMPLES

In the Sanātana Dharma there is no church with constitution and hierarchy in the accepted sense. But priests in the service of the religion together with numerous assistants are attached to each temple. Although no fixed hours and days are stipulated for worship in the sanctuaries, it is there, nevertheless, that most of the religious ceremonies take place. Consequently the temples are of considerable importance in the lives of the Hindus.

These buildings are sometimes so huge that they can contain a large number of pilgrims and travellers under their roof and, within their confines, several other buildings. In India every man is free to build a temple. No permission is necessary. Certain conditions must, however, be fulfilled with regard to orientation, situation, size and openings.

The Hindus possess some sanctuaries in which it is permitted to worship different gods and others, "empty" ones, where each person may invoke "his own iṣṭa". In addition altars may be found outside temples, on highways, under trees and at cross-roads. These statues of the divinity are placed out of devotion in such a way that passers-by may invoke them.

WORSHIP

The essential forms of worship are prayer and sacrifice. But the ritual proper to the cults, or pūjās, celebrated in the temples varies with the god to be worshipped. These pūjās may also be performed mentally (mānasapūjā), and yet have the same result. Interior worship (antaryāga) is the believer's quest for self-identification with the divinity. All Hindu rituals include study of the Sacred Books and offerings of gifts to images.

PRAYER

Prayer has its own laws and requirements. It is the concomitant of religious acts of sacrifice or offering.

The prayer or mantra is a "sacred formula" based upon the power of the word. Prayer, a sequence of syllables used towards specific ends, becomes efficacious only when it is pronounced with a rigorous observance of tone, rhythm and stress and is, in addition, preceded by the requisite mental concentration.

According to the Hindus, every being possesses in his unconscious mind a certain secret word, a key-word special to himself, which is revealed to him by his guru. This word—the root of the mantra combined with a mystic formula—makes up *his* mantra. The devout repetition of prayer is known as "japa".

By virtue of this repetition, it is possible to arouse extraordinary powers. On the physical plane the mantra can induce certain phenomena, and it can also lead to "liberation". On the spiritual plane, the effect is of a higher order and more subtle. Certain conditions are necessary for the correct recitation of mantras: a bath, clean clothes and hair, an empty stomach, calm surroundings, the smell of incense and the body in the lotus-posture (padmāsana). Without these preparations no results can be obtained. The great Bhaktas repeat their mantras the whole day long, even when travelling, walking or assisting at religious festivals, for they live in permanent contact with the divine. Śrī Ramakrishna was wont to claim that God's name and God himself are identical, so that the more his name is repeated, the sooner and more effectively is full realization of his presence attained. The believer repeats his mantras from a hundred and eight to a hundred thousand times at first as his guru directs. There are three ways of practising japa: by pronouncing (in a loud or a soft voice); mentally, though with a slight glottal contraction; or as a sort of mental prayer (without any accompanying physical reflex) conducive to complete concentration.

The mantras are sacred and constitute one of the greatest secrets of each man's life after his initiation. Their significance is esoteric and they open up for the initiate a whole field of spiritual meanings. Since, on the spiritual plane, they are a vehicle of human thought, they create for the reciter a peculiar atmosphere. Sound is perhaps as important as light for dispelling darkness and calling into action positive forces. Mantras are an indispensable part of ritual and of any form of religious discipline.

The sound "AUM" is the original mantra, the holy word made up of three syllables: AUM. It expresses the Trimūrti, or Hindu Trinity; Brahmā, the creator, Viṣṇu, the protector, and Śiva, the destroyer. In reality, these three are One.

SACRIFICE

Sacrifice is the religious act *par excellence*. It is an outward sign of adoration which takes the form of an offering to the divinity, an "oblation". The true nature of Vedic sacrifice is primarily a "self-dedication", the transposition from the secular into the sacred, which works a psychological change in the person who pays for the ceremony and ultimately affects the sacrificial objects, flowers, fruit, rice.

The whole of Vedic ritual was based upon the institution of fire. Fire serves as an intermediary between the celebrant and the deity. The function of sacrificial fire, first as the agent of purification and then as the vehicle by which sacrifice is offered, is of prime importance for the cult.

A distinction was drawn between "sacrifice involving only one fire" (the oldest form) proper to private ceremonies celebrated in the family hearth by the head of the family and "sacrifice involving three fires" which belongs to the solemn cult and especially to the sacrifice of soma (a rite which is practised less and less).

The hotṛ is "he who pours out" the oblation, the one who recites, to whose lot it falls to repeat the stanzas of the Rigveda whether in śāstra or in verses and isolated formulas.

SOLEMN RITES

Fundamental in the Vedic cult was the sacrifice of some, the basic sacrifice of its "Angel of Light". An important and detailed ritual lays down with precision the operations necessary to its preparation: the purchase, transportation, and measuring of the plant, the drawing of water to swell its stems, the submitting of the plant to pressure, the extraction of the sap and mixing with water, milk and sometimes honey. This ceremony is performed once a year. It lasts five days and ends with the offering to the gods of soma, which drink is considered as a purifying nectar conferring immortality.

If the celebrant is a Brāhman he tastes of the dishes offered and the rest of the officiants share what remains in a specified order. The scope of the sacrifice is wider than a lay person might imagine. The sacrificial formula brings with it an assimilation of strength, a veritable transubstantiation rather than a simple communion.

THE OFFERING

Generally speaking, in sacrifices, part of the offering is cast into the fire and part consumed by the officiants who, by this means, participate in the life of the gods. "Food is divine" is a fact upon which the Brāhmaṇas continually insist.

The gods must be offered whatever the individual values most. Produce from the land, milk, melted butter or "ghṛta", barley and rice (in cakes) are some of the gifts which the ritual specifies as offerings. Also necessary is incense and garlands of flowers symbolic of the benefits that the giver desires for the object of his veneration. Every god receives flowers especially consecrated to himself: Viṣṇu, white jasmine, Śiva, blue corolla and Kāli, scarlet hibiscus. The offerings may be strewn on the ground, in the air or on water. The "consecration" or dīkṣā precedes the soma sacrifice. The agnyādheya or "installation of the fire" is the prelude to all solemn ceremonies of the cult.

The Agnihotra, "fire-oblation", is one of the most important solemn rites. Every Brāhman who is head of a family or Vaiśya must perform it morning and evening, before or after sunrise and the appearance of the first star.

The Darśapūrṇamāsa or "sacrifice of the full and the new moon" lasts one day. The Aśvamedha or "sacrifice of the horse", one of the most impressive of all Vedic rites, represented the highest expression of royal authority. It is a soma sacrifice comprising a whole series of important sacrifices.

EXPIATION RITES

Together with the ritual, the Hindu religion possesses expiation ceremonies which were codified at the end of the Vedic period. These are ordinary or special oblations, sometimes ablutions, recitations or offerings intended to avoid the consequences of a fault or soiling. The expiatory rite may take the form of a gift, a religious endowment or it may be a work of piety accompanying the legal punishment of sinful action.

Errors may be involuntary and venial or they may be serious, of a religious nature, sometimes provoking expulsion from the caste. The idea of impurity is often inherent in these sins which are judged by an official castigator presiding over a miniature law court.

PRIVATE RITES

These rites are in accordance with the teachings of the Sūtras or Domestic Aphorisms. The daily rite of the saṁdhyā is the rite of the "junction" of day and night and replaces the ancient Agnihotra rite. It consists of an internal ablution followed by an aspersion of the head, then a recitation of the Gāyatrī which is a mantra from the Rigveda, in worship of the sun as it appears on the horizon. Then follow a fresh ablution and the recitation of the Gāyatrī and, after the prāṇāyāma, the repetition of more formulas or prayers and offerings. These rites are also observed at noon and in the evenings.

The five great daily sacrifices (mahāyajña) are:

1. the vaiśvadeva offered to "All the Gods" which is a fire oblation (homa) performed before the midday meal, using portions set aside from the meal;

2. the bali, a scattered oblation consecrated to the "beings";

3. the pitṛyajña or tarpana, a libation of water and sesamum which is offered to the Manes;

4. the atithi, a rite of hospitality towards visitors, especially ascetics;

5. the brahmayajña or recitation of a passage from the Veda.

Together with these rites should be counted the worship of the five protecting divinities (pañcāyatana): Viṣṇu, Śiva, Sūrya, Pārvatī, and Ganeśa who, symbolized by figurines, receive daily offerings in the home.

Collective agricultural rites are also current. These occur at the time of ploughing and of harvesting. The domestic hearth is a centre of religious life which is faithfully maintained from the marriage ceremony onwards.

THE SACRAMENTS OR SAṀSKĀRAS

Twelve principal sacraments[1] exist. First of all, birth. "By a son," says Manu, "worlds are conquered; by the son of the son, immortality is gained; by the grandson of a son, the world of the sun is obtained."

Birth is the occasion of a ceremony in which first of all a morsel of honey and clarified butter is inserted into the infant's mouth upon a golden spoon, after which occurs the "dedication of the child to Ṣaṣṭhī" the protecting goddess. The "giving of the name" occurs on the tenth day after birth.

Of greater importance is the Initiation which consecrates the child's entry into the Brāhmanic community and confers upon him the title of dvija, "twice-born". This ceremony takes place at eight to twelve years, according to caste, and brings with it the

[1] We use here the word "sacrament" in the general sense of "religious ceremony". Among Christians the word has a more precise meaning, namely, an outward sign ordained by Jesus Christ which effects what it signifies.

wearing of a holy thread made of three white cotton strands twisted together. The father appoints a guru and the child's studies begin. This very important sacrament is called the upanayana, while the birth ceremony is called the jātakarman and involves the lighting of a special fire, the smoke of which is allowed to spread. From birth to death the different stages of a Hindu's life are marked by ritual ceremonies.

MARRIAGE

A series of ritual practices also figures in the texts of Śruti (revelation) relating to marriage. By scrutinizing the stars the date of the ceremony may be determined, then, after the oblations, comes the rite of the "seven steps" which sanctions the irrevocability of marriage. In this ceremony the affianced bride steps upon a stone, turns all around the fire and makes the seven steps while holding her fiancé by his hand. For the major part of the ceremony the formulas are taken from the great Hymn to Sūrya.

FUNERAL CEREMONIES

Cremation is the customary form of funeral in India and is described in the texts. The funeral procession, preceded by torches, is accompanied by the relatives, and the body is borne by hand or upon a chariot to the place of cremation. The religious formulas exhort him who has abandoned his body to seek union with the Manes and with Yama. His body is exorcized of any demon and is placed upon the funeral pyre between the three fires. Prayers and offerings accompany the lighting of the fire. Purification rites for the family follow the ceremony.

The Srāddha completes the funeral ceremonies. This consists of making the preta ("the departed") into a pitṛ or "father", that is, an influential and well-disposed ancestor. In this rite water and balls of rice are placed on the ground for the dead man's use in the presence of three Brāhmans who represent the ancestors.

CHAPTER XIV

HOLY PLACES AND PILGRIMAGES

The holy places of India are innumerable and, however inaccessible, remain the object of assiduous pilgrimages. The pilgrims journey hundreds of miles on foot, singing sacred litanies on their way, in order to see some image of their god or obtain a "darśan" of him.

Pilgrims visit temples and holy places with immense fervour nor do they omit to offer up prayers in every sanctuary they pass, even if they have to go out of their way to visit a temple which is not that of their iṣṭa.

Water plays a great part in pilgrimage rites. To bathe in a sacred pool or river is the equivalent of a purification ceremony. The Ganges is pre-eminently sacred amongst rivers. It is said that where its course is invisible it touches heaven. Its waters, which flow down from mountain heights, have an unrivalled purifying efficacy and shallow steps or ghats lead down to that river, whose northern reaches, called the river Mandekini, are also a famous object of pilgrimage. The water of the Ganges is said by Rāmakṛṣṇa to be "as pure as Brahman". "Our mother Gaṅgā" as the river is called in India is, from its source in the Himalayas to its mouth in the Gulf of Bengal, paramount as the goal of pilgrims from all the sects of India. But some stretches have the right to be considered more holy than others. This is the case at Gaṅgotri, where the river leaves the Himalayas, at Hardwar with the temple of Gaṅgādvāra, at Prayāg on the confluence of the Ganges and the Jumna and finally Sagar island at the mouth.

The most sacred place of India is Benares, the great religious city with its 1,500 temples, which sees over a million pilgrims every year. It is a town of unique character. Every cult is represented there, though Benares is, in fact, sacred to Śiva. Any man that dies in Benares is automatically freed from the bonds of saṁsāra.

The most important towns after Benares that serve as centres for pilgrimage are seven in number: Hardwar, Ujjain, Mathura, Ayodhya, Dwarka and Conjeeveram. Puri, in Orissa, is the capital of the Vaiṣṇavas. Every year at monsoon time festivals follow one another closely and during this time the gigantic statue of the Juggernaut (Viṣṇu as master of the world; it is kept in the sanctuary of the vast temple) is carried about for several days in commemoration of Kṛṣṇa's journey from Gokula to Mathura. The statue is borne in an immense chariot drawn by thousands of pilgrims. Every pilgrim is obliged to accept the "prasād" or ritual food from whatever hand it is offered. Thus caste distinctions are swept away. It was to Puri that Śrī Caitanya came in the fifteenth century when he fell into ecstasy upon entering the sanctuary and there it was that he disappeared mysteriously.

Vrindavan and its neighbourhood are still renowned as a centre of pilgrimage. Here is the birthplace of Kṛṣṇa and the whole region is considered sacred territory. Its very atmosphere is special. It is said that "the air there is so charged with sanctity and spirituality that the world is forgotten in it. The water is sacred, sacred are the flowers, the insects, the buildings, and the very dust, for upon this dust the Lord has walked and danced. Everything here is conducive to the development of spiritual life and mystical experiences." It is the holy land of the cult of Kṛṣṇa and it attracts to it fervent pilgrimages every year.

Mathura, the religious capital of southern India, with its vast temple, draws huge crowds. It is open to all comers and even non-Hindus are allowed to assist at the sumptuous processions that take place there. The tīrtha or ford is a focal point of religious interest. Dedicated to particular ṛṣis, the tīrthas are to be found in the vicinity of lakes, rivers and so forth and always in association with a cult.

FESTIVALS

Religious festivals are made exceedingly frequent by the fact that every orthodox Hindu, whichever his chosen divinity, takes part in the feasts dedicated to all the other divinities for, in his eyes, they are all the same thing—a different aspect of the one god. The feast days are solemnized according to a strictly observed calendar. Among the best known is the Durgā-pūjā in October and November. An ancient text describes it as follows: "Upon a marvellous chariot, decked with fine linen and hung with mirrors and little bells, the idol of Durgā is carried. Maidens and women strew it the while with flowers, Durb grass, rice in the husk and water. The streets are watered and houses and doors are covered with canopies. No trees are felled and prisoners are set free."

The Śivarātrī or festival day of Śiva occurs every lunar month and is observed with even greater solemnity (mahāśivarātrī) in January–February. The Dīpāvalī (Divālī), as its name (array of lights) would suggest, is celebrated with the aid of lamps set out in places of both religious and non-religious importance. This is accompanied by public rejoicing (Renou).

The births of Kṛṣṇa and of Rāma are also celebrated. The chief Tamil feast is the Pongal (January–February). It consists of an offering to several divinities of rice boiled in milk and of aspersing cows which have been adorned with garlands. Afterwards the flocks are dispersed and allowed to graze at will, later to be reassembled and confronted with divine images which are carried in procession. Fast days generally precede these festivals.

THE PŪJĀ

Adoration of the image of a god is known as pūjā. Image-worship is very widespread among Hindus, although for most of them the image is only a material aid to adoration of the god and merely furthers the cult in the same way as prayers or other external religious practices.

Images are constructed according to rules laid down in treatises which specify even the minutest details: postures, attributes and colours representing the characteristics of each god. The installation of the idol in the temple involves a consecration accompanied by the rites of "the infusion of breath" and "the opening of the eyes".

The pūjā is a rite that is both private and public. As a solemn rite it takes place within the temple and varies according to the importance of the sanctuary and of the ceremony. It is celebrated by the priest attached to the holy place and the faithful confine themselves to making offerings and muttering mantras and invocations. By a succession of rites the image is bathed, dressed, adorned and perfumed; it is given to eat and drink; flowers are placed all about it and lights are swung. The image is now and again carried outside the temple and in these processions or yārās the divinity is installed in a monumental car and eventually immersed in some sacred lake or river.

It is necessary to read into this series of ritual actions the abstract symbolism of the godhead's "descent" into the image and of the divinity's personification being "invited to make itself present" and "to breathe itself into" the image (Herbert, *op. cit.*, p. 324).

Ritual cults may also be performed mentally and are then no less efficacious.

MONASTIC ORDERS

A Śaivite order was founded as early as about the ninth century. Its foundation is attributed to Śaṁkara, the great Vedāntist philosopher. This monastic order was made up of ten brotherhoods whose members were called Daśanāmins "those that have ten names" or again "the bearers of the stick with one knot".

Of the other religious orders, some were made up exclusively of Brāhmans. Others, on the contrary, were open to the four castes (only untouchables and outcasts were excluded). It is claimed that four monasteries were founded by Śaṁkara:

Sringeri in Mysore, Govardhana at Puri in Orissa, Sarada at Dwarka in Kathiawar and Joshi at Badarinath in the Himalayas. The head of the monastery at Sringeri wields an authority that stretches far beyond the adepts of his order and earns him the title of "master of the world".

Other brotherhoods also founded monasteries. The Vaiṣṇavas are responsible for several. The order of the Vairāgins of Rāmānanda is recruited from the śākta section of the community, whereas the saṁnyāsins of Rāmānuja consists of Brāhmans only. Monasteries also exist that have been founded by the sect of the Liṅgāyats and these have sent forth emissaries into every centre where this cult is represented.

THE SANĀTANA DHARMA TODAY

India throughout its history has poured out and continues to pour out an unending succession of great sages, true heirs and continuers of the ṛṣis of Vedic times. These holy men constitute an unbroken chain and their glory has sometimes spread even to the West. Some of them gathered about them disciples from many parts of India and even of the world who formed themselves into "āśrams" or communities without any intention of becoming new sects but of being rather centres of enlightenment.

At the end of the eighteenth century Ram Mohun Roy (1774–1833) made attempts towards religious unity. Although of orthodox Brāhman stock, Ram Mohun Roy was inspired by the purest Sufism and, thanks to his being of both Islamic and Indian culture, to his knowledge of Oriental and Western languages, which opened his eyes to all the trends of contemporary thought, he became one of the pioneers of the universal "idea" that was then beginning to take shape. He associated himself with no orthodoxy and declared himself to be a "unitarian". He worshipped a god who was one and invisible. He wanted to reinstate the true spirit of the Vedas while at the same time studying the Gospels. In 1828 he founded the "Brāhmo Samāj" or House of God, dedicated to the worship of Brahman one and without equal. He intended his church to be a universal house of prayer, open to all men without distinction of colour, caste, race or creed.

The Brāhmo Samāj, thanks to its adherents, survived its founder and later became merged with the group formed by Debendranath Tagore (an impressive mystical figure, father of Rabindranath Tagore) which was known as the Tattvabodhinī and was based on a specifically Hindu kind of monotheism.

In 1862, Keshub Chander Sen who, in his turn, took over the direction of the Brāhmo Samāj gave it such an energetic leadership that he endangered its existence. The seed sown was to germinate and bear, in India and elsewhere, that same fruit of the universality of faith. But a schism intervened and, in 1879, the Sādhāraṇasamāj or "common society" was founded under the presidency of Ananda Mohun Bose. Keshub Chander Sen then created, in 1881, the Nava Vidhāna or "new dispensation", a sect in the Christian style of which he declared himself the head. He died in 1884. As a religious figure he presented a certain complexity and he wanted to link the Christian message to his own faith and to prepare the way for bridging the gap between men. The internal struggle that he had to undergo made him on occasions incomprehensible to his followers "despite his limpid sincerity", as his friend Ramakrishna put it.

The Sādhāraṇasamāj is the only group whose importance resides more in the quality of mind of its adherents than in their number. Many other names deserve to be mentioned and very many more, that might otherwise figure amongst those of the most eminent saints, will remain for ever unknown.

Dayānanda Sarasvatī (1824–88), the Vedāntic ascetic, represents a fairly strong reaction against the previous movements, which he took to resisting violently with the intention of re-establishing the Vedic tradition at its most orthodox. With this view in mind, he created at Bombay in 1875 the Āryasamāj or "Aryan association". Although he gave a universalist form to his ideas, he was careful at the same time to preserve certain nationalistic trends.

Ramakrishna, born in Bengal in 1836, the son of a poor Brāhman, has a place among India's greatest mystics. By some he has been considered as an avatar.

His teaching was a Śaṁkaran Vedāntism, but he wished to know every path that leads to God. He examined them one after the other and was enriched by all his experiences. It could be said that he spent a part of his life in a state of ecstasy. An ardent Vaiṣṇava, Ramakrishna was especially attached to the cult of Kālī, the Mother, who for him was the Absolute, for he knew that all the differences separating men derive from the same mother, that the Omnipresent Differentiation is God's own face and that all religions lead to the same and Only God.

It was Vivekānanda (1863–1902), the disciple and spiritual successor of Ramakrishna, who founded the Order of Ramakrishna, which was composed of "svāmins" or masters. In 1897 this order took over the Ramakrishna Mission which was devoted to the performance of philanthropic works.

Vivekānanda, who took up his master's message in order to spread it throughout the world, presented at the Chicago Congress of Religions his theory of a universal religion "knowing no limits of time and space and combining all the creeds devised by the mind of man". This dogma is no other than that of man stamped with the divinity and of his limitless capacity for evolution. The memory of Vivekānanda, together with his aim of tolerance and universalism in religion, is kept alive at Belūr, near Calcutta. Margaret Noble as Sister Nivedita was one of Vivekānanda's earliest and greatest disciples.

Even more recently, Gandhi gave considerable prestige to religious tolerance by his whole life.

Ramaṇa Maharṣi, who died a few years ago, in 1950, lived at Tiruvanāmalai. His mystical experiences were the covering for an exceptional character. His attempt to live in the imagination the agonies of death led him to such a state of illumination that he seemed to belong no more to this world. Then he espoused silence, for "that consciousness of unity which alone matters" can only be communicated in silence. His spiritual influence was strong and durable.

Aurobindo Ghose or Śrī Aurobindo was born in Calcutta in 1872 and died in 1951. He was one of contemporary India's great religious thinkers as well as being a considerable scholar.

He was stirred by the appeal of the divine, practised Yoga and devoted himself to spiritual self-realization in his āśram at Pondichery. In 1914 he founded the review "Ārya" in which many of his works appeared. His research was particularly concerned with the Vedas, the Upaniṣads and the Gītā, for he claimed that the traditions of ancient India held the key whereby man might discover the true meaning, the whole meaning, of the "secret of the Veda".

SELECT BIBLIOGRAPHY

1. *Texts.*

Translations of many important texts are contained in:

MÜLLER, F. Max (Editor): *The Sacred Books of the East*, Oxford and New York, Oxford Univ. Press, 1879 onwards.

LANMAN, C. R. (Editor): *The Harvard Oriental Series*, Cambridge, Mass., Harvard University Press, 1891 onwards. (This series also contains works dealing with philosophy and literature.)

2. *Religion.*

MONIER-WILLIAMS, Monier: *Brāhmanism and Hindūism, or Religious Thought and Life in India*, London, John Murray, 1887.

3. *Literature.*

WINTERNITZ, M.: *A History of Indian Literature*, translated by S. Katkar and H. Kohn, volumes I and II, Calcutta, University Press, 1927–33.

KEITH, Arthur Berriedale: *A History of Sanskrit Literature*, Oxford and New York, Oxford Univ. Press, 1948.

MACDONNELL, Arthur A.: *A History of Sanskrit Literature*, London, William Heinemann, 1900.

4. *Philosophy.*

HIRIYANNA, M.: *The Essentials of Indian Philosophy*, London, Allen and Unwin, and New York, Macmillan, 1949.

CHATTERJEE, S., and DATTA, D.: *Introduction to Indian Philosophy*, Calcutta, University Press, 1950.

5. *History.*

Cambridge History of India, volumes I–VI, Cambridge and New York, Cambridge Univ. Press, 1922–53.

MAJUMDAR, R. C.: *An Advanced History of India*, London, Macmillan, and New York, St Martin's Press, 1950.

6. *Language.*

MACDONNELL, Arthur A.: *Sanskrit Grammar for Students*, Oxford and New York, Oxford Univ. Press, 1927.

WHITNEY, William Dwight: *A Sanskrit Grammar, including both the classical language and the older dialects, of Veda and Brāhmaṇa*, Cambridge, Mass., Harvard Univ. Press, 1950.